HOW TO PLANT A CHURCH

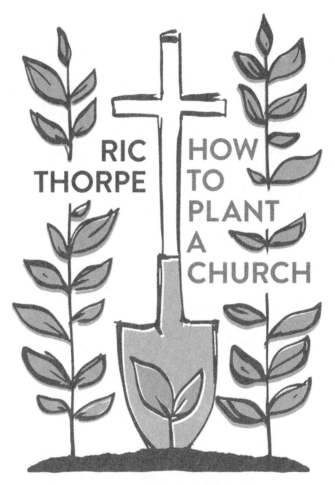

RIC
THORPE

HOW
TO
PLANT
A
CHURCH

A Guide to Planting Healthy
New Worshipping Communities

The Gregory Centre for Church Multiplication
ccx.org.uk

HOW TO PLANT A CHURCH

First published in 2024 by The Gregory Centre for Church Multiplication

The Old Deanery, 6 Dean's Ct, London EC4V 5AA

www.ccx.org.uk

Editor Helen Cockram

Cover Design by David Wardle

Typesetting and Layout by David McNeill, Revo Creative

ISBN 978-1-8384743-5-5

eISBN 978-1-8384743-6-2

Printed in the United Kingdom

First Edition 2024

1 2 3 4 5 6 7 8 9 10

Ever since the day of Pentecost, churches have been planted – without any exceptions, every church, in each locality across the world, has begun because of the combination of divine and human agency. Nearly 2,000 years on, planting churches continues to be the most wonderful way of proclaiming the good news and inviting new disciples to join The Way. But it's not easy – there is much to learn and plan and do and pray. There are few who are better guides to enable this than Ric Thorpe – not only does he have decades of experience and hard-won wisdom, but he has a heart which beats to see God's people partner with the Holy Spirit to embody and witness to Jesus' gift of life in its fullness.

MOST REVD AND RT HON JUSTIN WELBY, Archbishop of Canterbury

Ric's experience and profound study of church planting practice has made this an invaluable tool for anyone embarking on this vital element for the growth of the Church today. I couldn't recommend it more.

RT REVD SANDY MILLAR, Honorary Assistant Bishop, Diocese of Ipswich and St Edmundsbury and former Vicar of Holy Trinity Brompton' after Edmundsbury

In the 19th century, when the Church of England sought to expand into new territories, they often appointed a 'mission bishop' – an apostolic pioneer to lead the charge. Nine years ago, Ric Thorpe was called to such a role, initially focused on supporting church planting in London. He has since become nationally, ecumenically, and internationally recognised as an expert on church planting. When I have questions about church planting, Ric is the person I usually go to first. I can think of no one more qualified to teach us 'how to plant a church.'

REVD DR CHRISTIAN SELVARATNAM, Dean of Church Planting, St Hild College

This book is rich in practicalities, showing us how church planters can work within good financial, legal, safeguarding, and structural frameworks. It is also inspiring, full of stories of those who trusted God, heard the call to love and serve in a new place, and saw new communities growing to maturity in faith.

RT REVD DR JOANNE GRENFELL, Bishop of Stepney

From seasoned wisdom to personal anecdotes, Ric Thorpe's book is the companion I wish I had when embarking on my own planting journey – practical, profound, and deeply insightful.

REVD DR SARAH MCDONALD HADEN, Vicar of Cheltenham Network Church

Bishop Ric carries such a gentle, relational, strategic, prayer-fuelled approach to church planting. I am always keen to learn from him.

RT REVD DR JILL DUFF, Bishop of Lancaster

Few people know as much about church planting in an Anglican context as Bishop Ric Thorpe. A successful church planter himself, he has devoted passion and energy into helping the Church of England embrace it. I am so glad he has written this book.

REVD SARAH JACKSON, CEO of Revitalise Trust

Church plants are a vital part of a healthy mixed ecology of church life. But what does it take to plant and help them grow? This book is an invaluable answer to that question. With characteristically disarming style, Ric has produced a book all church planters, sending church leaders, and those who support them will need in their hands. It is a privileged insight into the fires of faith and purpose that have propelled a new form of leadership. And it offers a timely reminder of Christ's promise to build his Church, taking up the best of our efforts along the way.

REVD CANON DR MARK POWLEY, Archbishop's Mission Enabler for the North

A timely book confronting the very real challenges the established Church is facing. It's honest and rooted in the belief that God continues to build his Church.

FR ROSS GUNDERSON, Vicar of St Etheldreda with St Clements Church

CONTENTS

Resources

The Gregory Centre for Church Multiplication can help you reach new people in new and renewed ways, through planting, lay-planting, growing, pioneering and estates mission.

This book is just the start of a journey. For more information on how to plant a church, scan this QR code to be taken to a resourcing page from the Gregory Centre for Church Multiplication.

@The GregoryCCX

ACKNOWLEDGEMENTS

I owe a debt of gratitude to many friends, family, and colleagues who helped me on the journey of writing this book. It's been nine years in the making!

Thank you to Louie and our children Zoe, Barny, and Toby. They have been on the church planting journey from the start and are great at keeping me grounded! Louie inspires me to chase after Jesus and his kingdom every day, and I am so grateful for her strength, encouragement, and patience.

Thank you to the many Christian leaders who have contributed to this book. Thanks especially to Archbishop Stephen Cottrell for his encouraging foreword. Thank you to every church planter who gave me permission to use their stories. I am continually inspired by the way you have faithfully followed God's vision, through the highs and lows, and I have the great privilege of getting to tell your stories to teach others.

Thanks too to all the friends, colleagues, and mentors who have equipped and encouraged me on the journey of church planting. Bishop Sandy Millar, over the years you have poured time, love, and energy into me; anything I offer in this book is a reflection of the way you discipled me. Thank you to Nicky Gumbel, Miles Toulmin, Tricia Neill, Mark Elsdon-Dew, and Sarah Jackson for your friendship and pioneering work in church planting. Bishop Richard Chartres, thank you for believing in me. Philip James and the Vision and Strategy Team in Church House, you faithfully serve the Church of England behind the scenes, making it possible for others to fulfil their vision for church planting.

My church planting journey began properly when we planted from Holy Trinity Brompton (HTB) to St Paul's Shadwell. But we didn't do it alone. Thank you to everyone at St Paul's Shadwell, St Peter's Bethnal Green, All Hallows Bow, St Luke's Millwall, and Christchurch Spitalfields, for your faith, hope, and love, through which I learned so much about the craft of church planting.

Finally, I wish to thank those who helped me write the book. Beth Green helped me get thoughts onto paper with support from The Mercers' Company. The whole team at CCX have encouraged and supported me along the way. Thank you to those who read drafts of the book and offered incise feedback: Bishop Philip North, Christian Selvaratnam, Bishop Sandy Millar, Ross Gunderson, Mark Powley, Sarah McDonald Haden, H Miller, Paul Pavlou, Sally Baily, Marcus Walker, Toria Gray, Bishop Matthew Porter, John McGinley, and Phil Hoyle. I also wish to thank Jo Stockdale for copy-editing, Julia Barbour for proofreading, David Wardle for his cover design, David McNeill for his work on layout and building this book, Toria Gray for overseeing and organising the production, David Cornish for coordinating the design process, and Ryan Gilfeather for writing support. Special thanks are due to Helen Cockram, my editor, who helped my vision for this book into reality through countless hours of encouragement and editing, and also to Andrea Bleakley, whose tireless administrative support makes all things possible.

FOREWORD

STEPHEN COTTRELL,
ARCHBISHOP OF YORK

What an exciting book! This hopeful yet practical guide takes us from vision to implementation in nine steps, firmly rooted in Scripture and prayer, the practicality of taking people on the journey with you, and recognising your own authority (or rather submission) within the process.

This is a guide that is very much based on Bishop Ric's own personal experience of planting churches and working as a leader for the Gregory Centre for Church Multiplication. Throughout the practical guidance and solid engagement with Scripture and theology, runs his deep, faithful, and prayerful commitment to God's purpose for the Church.

At a time when many are despairing about the decline of the Church and decreasing attendance numbers, enthusiasm and commitment for God's mission is needed to breathe life into communities. Church planting, building on ancient traditions, is growing the kingdom of God and reaching those who have little or no knowledge of church or God. There are words of encouragement in this book for anyone who is interested in leading new worshipping communities, not only for those who are ordained.

Bishop Ric encourages seeds of hope to flourish into healthy communities. Taking us on a journey from prayer to vision to the practicalities of planning, context, authority, learning about leading yourself and leading others, and finally to resources and implementation, this is the outworking of God's invitation to build the kingdom of God and Jesus' instruction to his disciples to 'Go and make disciples of all nations, baptising them . . . and teaching them.'

We grapple with how to do this today: How do we grow new worshipping communities? How do we expand the kingdom of God? How do we give new expression to the Christian life?

To do any of this, 'we need to put ourselves in faith's way, utterly dependent on God,' as Bishop Ric puts it, because 'that is when exciting things begin to happen.'

All of us long for God's exciting things to happen. So if you're wondering how to be part of this, how to get started, and what to do next, then start here. With this book.

If you're already on the journey, read this book as a reminder of who it is God is calling you to be.

Combining biblical reflection, missional ecclesiology, and a deep understanding of people and context, this is a book that can be yeast in the dough of the Church, helping us to rise again. Rooted in hope, prayerful expectation, and hard-won experience, it can help our churches grow and multiply so that more people hear the good news of the gospel and become part of Christ's body, the Church.

INTRODUCTION

All over the world, church planting is extending the kingdom of God.

As I write this, I have just spoken to a church leader from East Anglia who is planting churches in people's homes and working with the local bishop, who wants to expand and multiply them across the diocese. The same day I heard the news of 21 baptisms in a church plant in London that I helped enable just four years ago – it started as a small group and has multiplied into a church which now uses three buildings and has 400 young, diverse people. I was also excited to hear about the progress of an Anglo-Catholic city-centre revitalisation in the North West of England. I have now just finished preparing for a gathering of diocesan church planting directors covering over half the dioceses of the country, working on plans to create thousands of new congregations and Christian communities of all shapes and sizes over the coming years. For me, this is not an unusual day. New people are encountering Jesus Christ through these new worshipping communities every day!

Church planting is needed more than ever. We are in a missionary situation in the UK. The institutional Church is in decades-long decline and the lack of young people going to church indicates they are virtually an unreached people group.[1] Church planting is not the only solution, but evidence from the past indicates that it strengthens parishes, injects fresh faith, and produces new vocations.[2] In the present, church revitalisations are turning declining churches into growing ones.[3] So I remain hopeful! Denominations, movements, and networks that are actively involved in church planting are growing.[4] In recognition of the way new churches and Fresh Expressions of Church were growing and impacting local churches across the nation, the Church of England's House of Bishops commended church planting in 2018, officially making it part of its DNA. In 2019, its General Synod encouraged

---

1 Church of England average weekly attendance was 654,000 in 2022, down from 854,000 in 2019. In 2022, only 157,000 of these people were under 18 and 350,000 were over 70.
2 Christian Selvaratnam, *Why Plant Churches? Theological and Practical Reasons* (Cambridge: Grove Books, 2023).
3 Tim Thorlby, *Love, Sweat and Tears: Church Planting in East London* (London: The Centre for Theology & Community, 2016).
4 See https://churchmodel.org.uk/2022/05/15/growth-decline-and-extinction-of-uk-churches/.

'every parish and diocese to be part of this movement of forming new disciples and new congregations through a contextual approach to mission with the unreached in their community.'[5] This ancient Church is opening its doors to a new movement of kingdom expansion.

This book is for those who want to join this kingdom-expanding movement, and it has grown out of two personal experiences.

The first is doing it myself. The Bishop of London invited me and my family to plant a church in East London. It was an exciting adventure for our family as we entrusted ourselves to God. The experience was daunting but exhilarating. It stretched us to our limits, but we saw the favour and generosity of God first-hand. I learned more about myself and more about what the Church could be, with a team of people committed to following Christ and seeing him transform that place. We made many mistakes and we learned even more. Through all of this, I began to reflect on how we could do this more effectively as we made plans to plant and revitalise other parish churches in Tower Hamlets. In the miracle of God, we saw people coming to faith, churches coming back to life, churches growing and impacting their communities, and the Church enjoying the favour of those in the community.

A second experience comes from my role as Bishop of Islington and Lead Bishop for Church Planting in the Church of England. As I have reflected on my own experiences, challenges, and lessons learned, more and more church planters have been sent our way for advice and training. Over the last 25 years, I have consulted with hundreds of church planters, of all traditions and contexts in the Church of England, and I have observed and learned from thousands more in other denominations across the world. That learning is continuing as I convene the National Church Planting Network – a group bringing together every denomination and church network actively involved in church planting in some way around the UK.

In 2015, we founded the Gregory Centre for Church Multiplication (CCX for short) which equips church leaders to plant new churches and support the growth of the Church in England and beyond. We now work with ordained and lay (those who are not ordained)[6] church

---

5 General Synod motion on A Mission-Shaped Church, GS2142, July 2019.
6 Lay, from the Greek *Laos* meaning 'people,' leaders are not ordained but have a calling to lead.

planters, mission directors in dioceses, and with bishops and their senior teams, both here in the UK and in a variety of contexts further afield. We developed the Plant Course to help church planting teams on their journey from initial vision to launch, and much of the material we use on that course is contained in these pages.[7]

This book is for people with a vision to plant a church. It is for anyone, anywhere, any tradition or size of church, lay or ordained, with any particular role. I acknowledge that I write from the perspective of someone rooted in the Charismatic-Evangelical tradition in the Church of England. I learned about church planting and became a planter myself in this context. Since then, in my role as a bishop, I have grown in my desire to see the whole Church involved in this work. I have learned much and been inspired by other traditions and their own histories of church planting, many of which have contributed to the key lessons in this book. My hope is that this book will inspire you and encourage you and equip you to join in with God's work of revitalising the Church and changing the world to be more as he intended it to be.

So, how do you plant a church? Like seeking counsel from those who have gone before, this book will guide you through the key questions you need to consider before you plant. We'll cover how to build a foundation of prayer, how to develop your vision, how to adapt to the context you're going to, and how to be sent well. We'll cover how to lead yourself and your team effectively, how to gather and manage your resources, and finally, how to launch your plant and multiply it. You can read it in a single sitting, or chapter by chapter with a team, or just dip into the parts that will help you most.

The beginning of any church plant starts with prayer.

7 Details about the Plant Course can be found at www.ccx.org.uk/plant.

1
PRAYER

HOW TO PREPARE THE GROUND FOR PLANTING

This is the most important chapter in this book. You'd expect me to say we need to pray. Prayer sets the content and approach of this book apart from any other start-up handbook. In a sense it is more about spirituality, encompassing every aspect of our relationship with God. Prayer engages the supernatural. Prayer says, this is of God. Prayer helps us see and know that we are merely mortal, whereas the one we pray to is immortal, invisible, God-only wise. Not only that, but when Jesus said in the Sermon on the Mount, 'When you pray . . .' his assumption is that of course we would be praying because we need to be communicating with God about this.[1] Prayer is a gift of the Holy Spirit. The Spirit dwells in our hearts, activating our relationship with God. It is through the Spirit that we are adopted as children of God, enabling us to cry out to him.[2] The Spirit teaches us what and how to pray. I have been learning about prayer for decades and he is still teaching me.

Tim Matthews, who led the church plant to Lovechurch Bournemouth, knew that prayer was essential: 'The first thing we did to prepare was pray. You don't want your church plant to be a work of human hands. It has to be born in adversity and prayer. You're all facing huge challenges: financially, relationally, and geographically, and so it has to begin with seeking God.'

Prayer puts you in the proper place before God, reminding you that it is his work through you. It leads you to continually seek his help. Prayer must be at the heart of any church plant and needs to be the heartbeat of every church planter. Once the church becomes established and mature, prayer will be one of the essential rhythms so it is vital to set prayer within the very DNA of the church from its conception. And there will be

1 Matthew 6:6.
2 Romans 8:28.

moments when the only way forwards is to fall on our knees and cry out to God for his divine intervention!

WHY PRAY?

It might be obvious, but I want to set out, for the avoidance of any doubt, the reasons why we need to pray about church planting. We pray because:

1. Jesus is the head of the Church

'God placed all things under his feet and appointed him to be head over everything for the church, which is his body, the fullness of him who fills everything in every way.'[3] He has full responsibility for the Church and he is in charge of it. Since he is head over everything for the Church, we must submit to his authority and oversight in every matter. We recognise that he is the one who is calling us to plant. And he is the one who delegates authority and responsibility to us for planting, leading, teaching, and pastoring it. Therefore it is good to talk to him about these things.

2. Jesus is building his Church

Jesus said to Peter that he would 'build my church.'[4] While we might be planting a church, it is actually Jesus who is building every person into it[5] and he alone is growing it. He is the true church planter and we are called to co-work with him. So we pray for Jesus to build his Church, for him to grow it, for him to strengthen it and watch over it.

3. Jesus will defend the Church

Jesus goes on to tell Peter that 'the gates of Hades will not overcome it.' For Jesus to say this shows us that he is expecting demonic challenges and that we should expect that too. We will go deeper on spiritual warfare in later chapters. But also we can be assured that as we look to Jesus, when there are troubles and challenges, he will not allow any demonic activity to overcome the Church. We should absolutely call out to Jesus to protect us and the Church in prayer.

3 Ephesians 1:22–3.
4 Matthew 16:18.
5 1 Peter 2:5.

4. Jesus will guide the Church

We need to ask for wisdom and discernment at every stage, not just proceed according to our own human instincts for what might work best. God loves to guide us when we ask him: 'The Lord will guide you always'[6] and, 'If any of you lacks wisdom, you should ask God, who gives generously to all without finding fault, and it will be given to you.'[7]

5. Jesus will provide for the Church

'God will meet all your needs.'[8] We need to remember that God alone provides the resources for the vision he gives. 'Ask and it will be given to you; seek and you will find; knock and the door will be opened to you. For everyone who asks receives; the one who seeks finds; and to the one who knocks, the door will be opened.'[9]

6. Jesus will raise up leaders for the Church

Many church leaders say they don't have enough leaders to take responsibility for church ministries. But have they prayed? Jesus invites us to ask for leaders: 'The harvest is plentiful but the workers are few. Ask the Lord of the harvest, therefore, to send out workers into his harvest field.'[10] We must pray for discernment to see the emerging leaders that Jesus is calling and then play our part to nurture them to maturity.[11]

7. Jesus brings in God's kingdom

When Jesus taught us how to pray, he began with, 'Your kingdom come.'[12] God longs for us to live in his kingdom both now and forever. He wants to transform communities around us, to make them places where people are filled with love for him and one another. We pray for God's kingdom to come because we know that when people are fired up with God's love, they bring his transforming life and power with them wherever they go and change the world around them.

6 Isaiah 58:11.
7 James 1:5.
8 Philippians 4:19.
9 Matthew 7:7–8.
10 Matthew 9:37–8.
11 Ephesians 4.
12 Matthew 6:9–13.

8. Jesus wants you and your team to thrive

There are moments when church planting is exhausting. In the place of prayer, we discover Jesus' invitation: 'Come to me, all you who are weary and burdened, and I will give you rest.'[13] Prayer joins us with Christ. He takes on our burdens and gives us the strength we need to go on.

9. Jesus wants you to grow to trust him

Jesus constantly invites us into a deeper trust in him. When things seem impossible, he says: 'What is impossible with man is possible with God.'[14] When you feel you can't do something, remember: 'I can do all this through him who gives me strength.'[15] When you can't go on, he says: 'My grace is sufficient.'[16]

10. Jesus wants to grow your church

Jesus' call to 'go and make disciples of all nations' shows his desire to grow his Church. With that call, he assures us of his presence: 'And surely I am with you always, to the very end of the age.'[17]

There are many more reasons why prayer is the most important thing we can do – perhaps this could be a sermon series! Prayer is the foundation of any church planting. What might it look like in practice?

THE PRAYER LIFE OF A CHURCH PLANTER

Church planting is one of the most challenging things I have ever done. I have been stretched out of my comfort zone multiple times, experienced highs and lows relationally, emotionally, mentally, physically, and spiritually, and learned more about myself – sometimes uncomfortably – than at any other time of my life. I have seen God do extraordinary things, often at the last minute, to bless the church. I have also experienced times

13 Matthew 11:28.
14 Luke 18:27.
15 Philippians 4:13.
16 2 Corinthians 12:9; Psalm 91:15.
17 Matthew 28:19–20.

of great closeness to God, and desert times that have tested me as never before. Whether you are the lead planter, a member of the team, or a supporter of the vision, there is nothing like a church plant to get us on our knees.

I want to focus here on the need to depend on God, as the leader, and to cultivate that in your church planting team. I'll address the spiritual health of the leader later on in the chapter on leading yourself.

Perhaps the most important thing I have realised in church planting is my utter dependence on God. I have found it too easy to get caught up in busyness, in getting stuff done, in making things appear polished and perfect. And yet the things that have been most profound have been when God has done something that only he could do. Whenever people come to Christ, while it is a huge privilege to be involved, it is obvious that only God can change a heart. But I also recognise that God has chosen to involve us. So if I don't step forward in faith, not much happens, but when I do, I see that Jesus is the one who is doing the transforming. My friend Greg Downes is a very gifted evangelist. He leads people to Christ almost every day. He would be the first to say that this is God's work through and through. But I also know that if he didn't strike up the conversations, and talk about Jesus directly, and offer to pray, then there would be no revelation and no conversion. We need to put ourselves in faith's way, utterly dependent on God, and that is when exciting things begin to happen.

Paul Pavlou, who planted into The Church of the Risen Christ, Wyken, expresses this need to depend on God through prayer. After five attempts at planting, Paul says that prayer was an essential part of his journey to plant the church he now leads in Coventry Diocese and that he learned from the experience. 'This job forces you on your knees in prayer, seeking out what God's will is. I probably wasn't doing that quite as I should have been before this job. Through the difficulties, and in hindsight, we've seen that God was working in us.'

Where are you in your prayer life? Do you have a spiritual director where you can unpack and reflect on your life with God? Underneath the soil you are cultivating, is there a bedrock of dependence on Jesus in a living and dynamic way? In Acts 13, the prophets and teachers of the church in Antioch prayed and fasted before sending Barnabas and Saul out on their first missionary journey. I too have found that at key moments in my life I have needed to set aside time to fast and spend significant time in prayer – usually I need to go away on my own, walking and reflecting, in quiet or crying out to God. Find your rhythm and approach – whether it is going to a retreat house or space on your own – so that you find that deeper connection with God, where you can draw on his rich resources and strength.

PREPARING THE GROUND

Ploughing up the ground is normal practice for farmers to get ready for sowing seeds. If you don't prepare the ground, nurture the soil, and sow seeds, there will be no harvest. 'Sluggards do not plough in season; so at harvest time they look but find nothing.'[18] Ploughing is a great metaphor for prayer. It is about preparing the ground to receive the seeds that will be sown. As Jesus taught in the parable of the sower, the 'seed falling on good soil' refers to someone who hears the word and understands it. This is the one who 'produces a crop, yielding a hundred, sixty or thirty times what was sown.'[19] Ploughing with prayer is as important for a church plant as it is for farming. How might we prepare our church plant with prayer?

At one of our early Multiply Church Planting Conferences, an annual event to encourage and equip church planters, Pastor Yemi Adedeji shared how the Redeemed Christian Church of God prepared for their church plants. As they had planted over 800 churches across the UK in 15 years, we were hungry to learn from them. They didn't major on strategy and in-depth planning, they focused on prayer. Six months before a plant was due to be launched, they sent a small team of people to pray in the city or town. That team would rent an apartment and invest hours, days, and weeks in intercessory prayer. They would walk the streets praying. They went to the council offices, the police stations, the magistrates' courts, the business parks, the school gates, and other important locations to pray. Their agenda was simple: they prayed 'your kingdom come;' they prayed the Lord's Prayer; they prayed for the well-being of the city; they prayed for God to bless the city; they prayed for people to come to Christ; they prayed for favour and success for the church plant.[20] It was a huge investment of

18 Proverbs 20:4.
19 Matthew 13:23.
20 Matthew 6:9–13; Jeremiah 29:7.

time and resources and demonstrates how they value the importance of prayer. Advanced and organised prayer will be key to preparation.

At St Paul's Shadwell, I was so grateful to Kerst Sikkema, a Dutchman, who God brought to join our initial planting team. He was a worship leader, songwriter, and intercessor and took a lead with intercession in the church. As we prepared for our first church plants from there, Kerst led small teams of intercessors on prayer-walks around the neighbourhoods that our bishop had suggested and where we felt God calling us. I remember one of his feedback reports where he said that God had given them two different phrases, one for each of the locations we were exploring: 'business as usual' and 'slow burn.' We were anticipating doing the same process for each plant, but here we felt God leading us to plan each one differently. This really helped us as we explored the implications. The first approach was to be one that we had done ourselves five years earlier, sending a team of 20 led by our curate and his family – 'business as usual.' The second would require a much slower approach, recruiting a planter from outside our parish and seeing people gradually join the plant over the next year – 'slow burn' – and this turned out to be what happened in practice and a much wiser approach. Prayer-walking is a great strategy to plan for.

Beatrice Smith, who planted Restoration Church, Tameside, used prayer-running to prepare the ground for the plant. Tameside borough sits on the eastern edge of Greater Manchester, an area some locals describe as 'forgotten,' where business closures are more common than openings. Beatrice felt a call from God that he would grow good things in the area, and birth something new. She moved to Tameside with her husband in 2012 in the hope of planting a worshipping community, but no avenues emerged. Beatrice felt she should prayer-walk – but began prayer-running, as walking felt too slow! As she ran the area, she asked God why he sent her, what he wanted for Tameside. She received a picture of a dry, cracked land, and felt that God knew just where he had placed her, and that he would revitalise that barren land. Years later, after no church plant had emerged, she met to pray with others who had a heart for Tameside. Someone shared an image of seeing a dry, cracked land, from which shoots were beginning to emerge, slowly growing into great oak trees. Beatrice felt seen and known by God, that his work might be gradual but he was faithful to what he had shown her years before.

She continued this prayer running for close to a decade before she was introduced to the team with which she would then plant Restoration Church. Like Beatrice, it might take a long time to prepare the ground for your plant, but it is important and necessary work!

A verse I was encouraged to learn as a young Christian was God's phone number: 33-3. It's actually Jeremiah 33 verse 3 which says, 'Call to me and I will answer you and tell you great and unsearchable things you do not know.' God wants us to call out to him, and he longs to speak to us, to reveal things to us, things that we could not possibly know but for him. I have found that going into prayer expecting him to speak leads to a more likely experience of hearing him speak. For that reason, it is helpful to record prayers and write down any Scriptures, words, or pictures that might have been heard and shared. This is a helpful way to weigh and discern prophecy over time (see 1 Thessalonians 5:19–22) and to reflect on what God might be wanting to say specifically about your particular circumstances. One of the ways we knew God was calling us to plant not just once, but many times, was through a continual stream of pictures and words in the same direction. That changed our posture towards being a church not just for the parish but being a resource for other churches and for the borough and beyond.

Andy Wilson is a licensed lay minister with the Church Army. Sensing a call from God, Andy and his family moved to Gloucester and started Share Matson in August 2019. Andy had felt a call to reach out to those in the Matson area that would never walk into a traditional church, to let them know God loved them and cared about them. Andy spent four months prayer-walking the area, both to help him become familiar with its community and to listen to God's heart for it. As he prayed, three words came back to him again and again during these months: serve, honour, and influence. Andy felt this was God calling him to come and serve the area, that out of that service he would honour them, and they would honour him, and from there influence would come.

When you're in your time of preparation, gather your sending team and ask, 'Are we preparing the ground well?' Share what you are doing individually and reflect on your prayer as a group. You may wish to dig deeper into your prayers of preparation with regular team prayer meetings, a team retreat, or prayer-walking around the planting location.

MAINTAINING HEALTHY SOIL

Once the soil is ploughed, it needs to be looked after so it is healthy and fertile for growth and harvesting. Regular corporate prayer needs to be the hallmark of any church. A church plant needs to establish this practice from the very beginning of its life. This keeps the church focused and dependent on God at every moment.

For our plant to Shadwell, we had fortnightly prayer gatherings where the emerging team prayed, and once we arrived, this became a weekly early morning prayer meeting. Jeremy Jennings was the prayer leader for many years at HTB, leading regular corporate prayer meetings for the church, and all the leaders I know from that church would point to those meetings as being the single-most important factor in all that God has blessed the church with over recent years. IMPRINT Church at Bank in the City of London is the church I referred to in my introduction, where there were 21 baptisms recently. That had been preceded by a 21-day fast that the whole church embarked on, with half their number gathering to pray online at 6 a.m. every morning. Prayer and fruitfulness are clearly linked.

It will look different for every church. The important thing is that we pray together. And that this becomes a culture in the life of the church. There are no shortcuts and this culture needs to be led by the leader of the church.

PROTECTING THE PLANT

A word about spiritual warfare – that is, the sense that when doing spiritual work it feels contested in particular ways, and what the apostle Paul called 'the devil's schemes.'[21] In our own church plant, we experienced many adverse growing conditions – sickness in the leadership team, a local issue with a tenant which turned nasty, gangs outside the garden, our son was mugged twice, Louie had stones thrown at her when she went out for a run. Some of this felt like spiritual warfare, in among all the blessings and growth that was happening. We may need to learn to pray in a different way – the early churches were warned to put on their 'spiritual armour' to protect us from evil and to guard against all kinds

---

21 Ephesians 6:11.

of cults, sorcery, idolatry, and worship of other gods.[22] How should we face this today? There are two schools of thought. The first is to pray with intention against the work of the devil and to storm the gates of hell. The second is to preach the gospel and get on with the evangelistic, teaching, and pastoral work we are called to do. Personally, I lean more to the latter, but the issues at stake are very real.

The Psalms are a deep resource for spiritual warfare as King David and the other psalmists wrestled with physical and spiritual enemies. The Anglican Prayer Book is another powerful resource. I have used the Third Collect in Evening Prayer, *for Aid against all Perils,* on many occasions: 'Lighten our darkness, Lord, we pray, and in your great mercy defend us from all perils and dangers of this night.'[23]

Remind yourself and the team regularly of who you belong to – you are on God's mission, his Holy Spirit is at work, he will guide you, and you need not fear. 'Do not be anxious about anything, but in every situation, by prayer and petition, with thanksgiving, present your requests to God. And the peace of God, which transcends all understanding, will guard your hearts and your minds in Christ Jesus.'[24]

A HEALTHY ECOSYSTEM OF PRAYER

As more and more church planting and evangelistic mission work is going on, there is a need not just for local prayer and the equipping of leaders to galvanise prayer in their church communities. There is also a need to pray at a wider level, strategically, regionally, and nationally, as Paul prayed for all the early churches, wrestling day and night in prayer.

I value more than ever the cycles of prayer that are built into our diocesan structures, where cathedrals and parishes cover each church in their diocese in prayer at least once a year. I value the prayer movements like 24-7 Prayer, Prayer for London, Thy Kingdom Come, and other networks who pray and prayer-walk and intercede for our cities, towns, and villages, and the Church in this nation. You could galvanise your prayer networks by asking local churches, cathedral, and monastic

---

22 Ephesians 6:10–20; Acts 19-20.
23 https://www.churchofengland.org/prayer-and-worship/worship-texts-and-resources/ common-worship/daily-prayer/morning-and-evening#mm8c.
24 Philippians 4:6–7.

communities to pray for you in their regular intercessions, asking your bishop and archdeacons to hold you in prayer, or to send out a newsletter to friends and churches in your networks to ask for prayer.

VISION AND PRAYER

St Paul encourages the Thessalonian church to do three things all the time: 'Rejoice always, pray continually, give thanks in all circumstances; for this is God's will for you in Christ Jesus.'[25] Prayer undergirded Paul's vision for the Thessalonian church. Prayer and vision are inseparable because they are so intertwined. As we pray for our church plant, our vision begins to emerge. As we pray, we begin to reflect on and work out where our vision is founded, theologically, historically, and personally. This combination of prayer and vision will give us a solid foundation on which to build.

25 1 Thessalonians 5:16–18.

CALL TO ACTION: PRAYER

At the end of each chapter, I will offer a 'call to action.' Many of these follow the responses we call for on the Plant Course. These actions are not exhaustive but will give you some next steps to apply straight away as you begin to discern the shape of the new Christian community that God is calling you to plant.

Explore these questions as you build your prayer strategy:

- Which disciplines of prayer are best for you and your team? Which do you want to build into your culture?
- How can you help your personal prayer life and your team's personal prayer lives to be intentional and accountable?
- Prayer-walking often leads to breakthrough in an area. How can you timetable prayer-walking for yourself and your team, and build a culture of it within your plant?
- Church planting is a very busy time. How can you ensure prayer isn't overtaken by activity?
- Who will you ask to pray for you? What tools will you use?
- If you don't give intercessors something to pray for they will pray for something else – how will you communicate prayer requests and answers?

2
VISION

HOW TO DEVELOP A COMPELLING VISION

Adventures are born in our imagination. We see something that might be. We feel a future that could be better. We hear a description that lights up our hearts. We know change is needed and the only way it will change is if someone does something about it. At that point, the called and courageous step forwards and say, 'I'll do it. Count me in. Send me.'[1] Then the adventure begins.

Vision is the visual description of that better future. Describing it will add depth and shape and colour to make it attractive. That description must be so compelling that it moves us to leave the comfort of our current status quo to the discomfort of tackling the changes needed in order to see that vision become a reality. It might involve making huge sacrifices and taking enormous personal risks. If the vision is attractive and worthy enough, it will be worth the cost. And there will be moments when those sacrifices and risks make us ask, 'Why am I doing this?' If we are to avoid things unravelling along the way, we need to be sure of the 'why' of our vision, and to be able to clarify and simplify it for others.

Experienced fishermen cast their fishing nets in such a way as to maximise the catch of fish. They have practised and honed their skills to achieve the best results. We need to learn to cast the vision we have been given if we want others to support us in any way, whether it is joining the team, or to give or pray for the venture. Casting that vision will involve telling it in many different ways, to appeal to different kinds of people, in order to achieve that goal. For planting churches and starting new worshipping communities, that will involve addressing many different questions from the outset. What are we actually trying to do?

1 See Isaiah 6:8.

What difference will it make? How does this fit within God's purposes as revealed in the Scriptures? Has this been done before in our own context? Do we have some kind of track record that we can learn from? How will we go about doing this? What values might underpin the journey towards our goal?

The goal of articulating and casting the vision for planting a church underpins everything else in actually doing it. It will be discerned and activated in prayer; it will involve planning and understanding where it fits in the wider Church's work; it will involve choosing the right team and understanding what kind of church the context requires; and it will need to be reiterated again and again as the vision is implemented to become a reality. So here are the elements I think are vital to include as you consider your vision.

Figure 1: There are many layers involved in a vision for a church plant

FOUNDED THEOLOGICALLY

You won't find the phrase 'church planting' in the Bible, but its practice is seen throughout the New Testament.[2] Church planting uses horticultural language for the creation of new churches and new worshipping communities. Jesus spoke about scattering seeds as a metaphor for the Word of God touching people's lives; about a mustard seed growing into a huge plant for the growth of the kingdom; and the multiplication of seeds, 30, 60, or 100-fold when planted in fertile soil for kingdom impact. The apostle Paul picks up this theme when he writes to the Corinthian church about its formation; he says that he planted the seed, Apollos watered it, but God made it grow.[3] 'Church planting' as a term emerges from this set of words and images. The emergence of new churches is described directly in the book of the Acts in Galatia, Greece, and Asia Minor, and indirectly in many of the New Testament letters as Paul, Peter, and John write letters to specific churches in specific places.

This missional impulse is part of the very nature of God. God is love, in every aspect of his being: 'God so loved the world that he gave his one and only Son, that whoever believes in him shall not perish but have eternal life.'[4] The ultimate act of Jesus loving us was to go to the cross, to bear our sins on his shoulders, and to die for us, taking the punishment that we deserve: 'But God demonstrates his own love for us in this: while we were still sinners, Christ died for us.'[5] After the resurrection, Jesus commissioned his disciples with a great task that would go through the generations, right up to today: 'Therefore go and make disciples of all nations, baptising them in the name of the Father and of the Son and of the Holy Spirit, and teaching them to obey everything I have commanded you.'[6]

As we unpack this verse a little further, we discover some interesting insights.

---

2 See Christian Selvaratnam's discussion of the term *Plantatio Ecclesiae* as a long-standing historic term in his book *The Craft of Church Planting: Exploring the Lost Wisdom of Apprenticeship* (London: SCM, 2022).
3 1 Corinthians 3:6.
4 John 3:16.
5 Romans 5:8.
6 Matthew 28:19–20.

1. **Go** – Jesus calls those who follow him to 'go.' We are to go to others, not expect them to come to us. They might be in our town, on our street, living next door, and we are to go to them – otherwise how will they ever hear about Jesus?[7]

2. **make disciples** – We are not just to be disciples, but to help others become disciples, to 'make' disciples. This involves actively helping, supporting, encouraging, and exhorting those people to follow Jesus themselves. Part of that is encouraging them to be witnesses themselves and make disciples of others. It is thus a multiplying movement of making disciples who make disciples who make disciples.

3. **of all nations** – The word 'nations' is *ethnē* in the original Greek, and here means people groups, understood to mean cultural, linguistic, or geographic groupings of people. In our increasingly diverse culture, we have many *ethnē* on our doorsteps and neighbourhoods. 'All' for Matthew means Jews and Gentiles, representing the whole of humanity. All are included in the missionary call.

4. **baptising them** – We are to welcome them into the Christian faith and the Church with the outward sign of baptism.

5. **and teaching them** – We are to teach these new disciples the faith that we have received, described in the Scriptures, formed as doctrines by the Church over the ages, and passed on through the generations, to us.

Baptism and teaching are activities associated with the Church – baptism initiates disciples into the Church, and teaching strengthens and deepens disciples within the Church. For me, this association is a strong affirmation of church planting and the creation of new Christian communities – going to new places, reaching new people with the good news about Jesus, making disciples, and establishing them in new churches where they too can be baptised and taught to follow Jesus.

Luke reaffirms Jesus' commission at the beginning of the Acts of the Apostles, calling his disciples to a growing, expanding mission, witnessing to the world about him: 'You will receive power when the Holy Spirit comes on you; and you will be my witnesses in Jerusalem, and in all Judea

7 See Romans 10:13–15.

and Samaria, and to the ends of the earth.'[8] Jerusalem was where the disciples were already, so they were to keep witnessing where they were to the people around them. Judea was the neighbouring region, similar culturally to Jerusalem. They were to go to them too. Samaria, though nearby, was different in culture and religion, and Jesus included them in his missionary call to the disciples. But his call went even further, 'to the ends of the earth,' to tell of his saving power. The call to witness, to go and make disciples, is universal, and starts where we are.

Having a theological vision for church planting underpins everything else. Every church that is planted comes from this original theological vision. When a church grasps this, they are open to the call of God to form a new church in new ways to reach new people. Church planting renews the whole church because the sending church is responding to the call to release and support those who are going. And, those who go, innovate and develop a church to contextualise this theological vision in a new way, which renews the whole church too. This supports our calling to reach all people everywhere – geographically, socially, and culturally. What might God be calling you to do?

VISION SHAPED BY HISTORY

Every church was a church plant once. Archbishop Stephen Cottrell says: 'Every church owed its existence to the dedicated ministry of a particular group of Christians at a particular time who were seeking to respond to the needs and challenges of their day by establishing some new expression of Christian life.'[9] So if we were to consider why and how our churches were originally planted, sometimes centuries ago, there is much we can reflect on and learn when we seek to plant churches today. In the UK, there is a certain credibility with a historical precedent, which helps bring more trust to its practice, even if we don't necessarily understand or have experience of what is being proposed. Others have done deeper, more in-depth studies of church planting throughout history, but here follows my whistle-stop tour of the history of church planting in England.

8 Acts 1:8.
9 Stephen Cottrell, 'Letting Your Actions Do The Talking: Mission and The Catholic Tradition,' in *Ancient Faith, Future Mission: Fresh Expressions in the Sacramental Tradition*, edited by Stephen Croft, Ian Mobsby, and Stephanie Spellers (New York: Seabury Books, 2010), 72.

Churches were first planted in England by Christians who accompanied the Roman invaders over the first two or three centuries. It is not clear to me whether there was anything systematic about how they came to exist, or how intentional they were about creating new churches – there simply isn't enough evidence. What is clearer is that there were two broad church planting movements that started in the sixth and seventh centuries, one from the South, through Augustine of Canterbury, the other from the North, through Aidan of Iona.

Pope Gregory sent Augustine with a small group of monks on a mission from Rome to convert the English in 597. In spite of initial fears, Augustine met with considerable local success, seeing Æthelbert, King of Kent, and most of his court converted and baptised. By Christmas 597, he is said to have baptised over ten thousand converts.[10] From his base in Canterbury, Augustine built Christ Church where he based himself. He then established the monastery of St Peter and St Paul and planted a number of churches around Kent. From there, missionaries and mission bishops evangelised London, Northumbria, and East Anglia with varying levels of success, making disciples and planting churches.

Meanwhile, the newly converted Christian King of Northumbria, Oswald, sent to Iona for a bishop to evangelise his people in 634. Aidan arrived in Lindisfarne and from there evangelised the North of England, preaching, baptising, and ordaining, often accompanied by the king. As the missionaries went out, they made disciples and planted churches. More monasteries were established, which became bases from which missionaries and church planters were sent to establish the Church in new places.[11]

In 633, Abbess Hilda hosted the Synod of Whitby at her monastery with bishops and senior church leaders from around England to bring a unified direction. It was ultimately decided to favour the Roman Church and its structures, bringing clear organisation, with hierarchy and demarcated geographic areas, to help focus evangelistic and pastoral work. Monasteries and minsters were evangelistic mission hubs from which bishops led teams of evangelists to witness to new peoples and

10 John R. H. Moorman, *A History of the Church in England* (Harrisburg: Morehouse Publishing, 1980), 14.
11 Bede, *The Ecclesiastical History of the English People*, edited by Judith McClure and Roger Collins, translated by Bertram Colgrave (Oxford: Oxford University Press, 2008), 113; Moorman, *History of the Church*, 17–18.

places, planting churches and Christian communities throughout the regions around them.[12]

Over the next few centuries, more and more churches were planted so that each city, town, and village community had its own church. The parish system in England organised these churches into dioceses and deaneries so that every person nominally belonged to a parish that was served by its own local church. Various additional types of church buildings were made to support community or individual needs – like chapels of ease and chantry chapels. Church attendance rose and fell through the centuries, depending on the spiritual climate. The Reformation led to many new denominations being formed and this consequently led to many new churches being created with buildings to house them.

A notable rise in planting new churches came during the Industrial Revolution, as people migrated from the countryside to cities for work. Churches of all denominations grew within the burgeoning populations of cities and market towns. For example, church members at St Mary Islington, near where I live, were determined to build new churches in the borough to match the fast population growth. Between 1828 and 1895, 38 churches were planted from St Mary's, aided by the creation of a Church Extension Society that raised the funds needed to build what was required.[13] Around the same time, the Oxford Movement was in full swing. Anglo-Catholic clergy went out from Oxford to establish beautiful churches in impoverished communities which had so far been neglected by the Church of England. Another movement of church planting a century later was the so-called 'daughter church' movement, which saw some parish populations extended through new housing in the post-war period. Some 800 new churches were created to reach and care for these new people with the gospel.

The widespread charismatic renewal of the Church in the 1960s and 1970s led to the British New Church Movement, where around 15 per cent of congregations left historic denominations to form around 300 new

12 George Hunter, *The Celtic Way of Evangelism: How Christianity Can Reach the West Again* (Oxford: Abingdon Press, 2000), 27; John Finney, *Recovering the Past* (London: Darton, Longman & Todd, 2011), 113.
13 Islington Church Extension Society, *Church Extension, Report of Proceedings at the Inaugural Meeting of the Islington Church Extension Society* (London: Seeley, Jackson & Halliday, 1857), 15.

churches, but they began planting and multiplied from the beginning.[14] An influential group of new or 'emerging' churches was the Vineyard Movement, comprising 2,400 affiliated churches worldwide, with over a hundred churches planted in England from their first church in Wimbledon, South West London in 1987. A number of Anglican churches began to be more intentional about church planting in this period, including HTB, which has initiated more than 35 direct church plants since 1985, with many granddaughter and great-granddaughter plants. It is a remarkable story of intentional church planting over a generation. And this is where my personal interest lies – St Paul's Shadwell was one of those plants from which many of my own lessons were learned.

The *Breaking New Ground: Church Planting in the Church of England* report, published in 1994, was the first formal document in which the Church of England accepted 'planting' as a missionary strategy.[15] Where this report saw church planting as 'a supplementary strategy that enhances the essential thrust of the parish principle,' a decade later the *Mission-Shaped Church* report stated that this was no longer enough.[16] 'No one strategy will be adequate to fulfil the Anglican incarnational principle in Britain today.' The latter report drew attention to Fresh Expressions of Church that were beginning to multiply all over the country, in different denominations and contexts. Fresh Expressions covers a multiplicity of models that favour a contextual approach to the formation of new churches. We'll explore this further in chapter 4 on Context.

Resource churches in the Church of England are an example of church planting and revitalisations in the first decades of this century. I have written elsewhere that they have their roots in the minster churches of the medieval period in England, and their practices follow patterns that we see in English Church history over the centuries.[17]

Today, the national Church of England's Vision and Strategy aims to

14 Max Turner, 'Ecclesiology In The Major "Apostolic" Restorationist Churches In The United Kingdom,' *Vox Evangelica* 19 (1989), 84.
15 Church of England, *Breaking New Ground: Church Planting in the Church of England* (London: Church House Publishing, 1994).
16 Graham Cray et al., *Mission-Shaped Church: Church Planting and Fresh Expressions of Church in a Changing Context* (London: Church House Publishing, 2004).
17 A resource church is designated by its bishop to be a church-planting church which trains its leaders to resource and support mission across a diocese. Ric Thorpe, *Resource Churches* (London: CCX, 2021), 9–12, 53–61.

be 'a church where "mixed ecology" is the norm, where every person in England has access to an enriching and compelling community of faith, by adding new churches and new forms of Church to our parishes, cathedrals, schools and chaplaincies.' The 'mixed ecology' is a horticultural term which describes lots of different kinds of church plants and mission approaches. This includes church planting, fresh expressions of church, chaplaincies, and online churches. It is a vision for every parish church to get involved in to reach new people in their parishes in a range of different ways. Across England, there are 12,500 parishes; if, say, 80 per cent of those were to become involved in this vision, that would add up to 10,000 new Christian communities being planted!

Added to this ambitious goal, naturally other denominations have church planting plans of their own, amounting to an exciting number of potential church plants. I hope this book will be a timely resource for these new leaders across the country, to equip and to encourage.

YOUR CONTEXTUAL AND PERSONAL VISION

Perhaps God is calling you to get involved in this movement of planting churches and new Christian communities. What is your vision? How do you work it out? Having a theological vision is an important foundation, and having a grasp of the historical foundations of church planting in this country is, I hope, encouraging too. But it needs something more specific and grounded for it to be meaningful and compelling if you are to embark on this adventure, and especially if you are to encourage others to join you. That will be related to the place you are going to – your context – and who you are as a unique individual or as a married couple or a group discerning the vision together.

1. It starts with a spark

Vision forming is a process that takes time. It's different for everyone. It may start with a flicker of an idea or a fully formed impression or a deep longing in your soul for people to know Jesus, but it takes time to get that picture from inside your head and heart to the people who are going to help make it happen. In my personal experience, we found that it starts with a spark – an idea that sets our imaginations ablaze. To make a fire, you need some fuel and then a spark or flame to set the fuel alight. The vision is the fire that needs a spark to get it going. And throughout, we need the Holy Spirit to help us to discern the vision as it forms. That spark can come from a number of places:

- **Scripture** – As we considered a church plant to Shadwell, which is on a busy road called The Highway, it was reading the prophecy in Isaiah 35 about a 'highway of holiness' where 'the desert and the parched land will be glad; the wilderness will rejoice and blossom' that began to stir within us.

- **Prayer** – As my wife Louie and I prayed and journalled together, we realised with awe and tears that God was calling us to be part of this new plant. In prayer, God speaks to us.

- **Life experiences and personal connections** – One of the things that guided us to Shadwell was that the church is known as 'The Church of Sea Captains' because it served the dock community in the 17th, 18th, and 19th centuries and has 70 sea captains buried in the churchyard. My father was in the Royal Navy and many of my relatives served on ships, and Louie has a portrait of an ancestor who was a merchant sea captain – it's hanging in our dining room. It was a wonderful connection and a fun confirmation for us. As we explored the local historic docks around Shadwell, it became clear that the vision involved reconnecting with the dock community – where once it was a church reaching out to the shipping community in Shadwell and Wapping, the new community who lived there were part of London's newly developing Docklands, with the Canary Wharf tower as its iconic symbol. This was the community that had to be reached with the gospel in this new generation.

- **People** – Some people will encourage us and fan the flame of the vision, adding colour and making it brighter. Others might push back against some of the emerging ideas – a dissenting voice or a spanner in the works – but these can often give boundaries to ideas and identify areas which need caution and care. They provide a sense of reality to the wild dreams we might have. Both voices are needed in the early days of a forming vision.

- **Seeing the need** – The spark for some comes from seeing the need in a place or with a people group. As they see the need, the Holy Spirit begins to burn within them and they realise that they are being called to address it.

- **Prophecy** – God speaking to our imaginations in pictures and stories can be key to the formation and development of a vision. An old friend shared an image he had had while praying for us of a ship tying up against a dock, unloading much needed supplies and seeing them distributed from there. He didn't know that the churchyard opened out to one of the old London docks. Soon afterwards, we discovered an old photo of a merchant ship unloading its supplies with the church in the background. It reaffirmed our sense that God was encouraging us to receive and give away his love and resources to the wider area beyond us. There were many other Scriptures and pictures that people gave us that continued to encourage and strengthen our calling to that place.

- **Passion** – Do you sense a growing passion for this call? For me, it grew over several years. There were setbacks along the way, and at times it felt like we faced dead ends and discouragement. But over time, it grew and grew, sometimes with tears, sometimes with deep urgency. What might be stirring within you?

These are the sparks that begin to shape our vision. They begin to show an outline, a purpose, a desire to see change, whether through prayer, or our personal experiences, or our circumstances, or the people around us, or through the prophetic. Once the spark of an idea is there, it can be fanned into flame.

2. Fan the vision into flame

The next stage is where the vision begins to take shape. All kinds of images and thoughts begin to bubble up around the initial idea and these need to be considered in a way that helps the vision to grow. The prophet Habakkuk is told by God to write down his vision: 'Write down the revelation and make it plain on tablets so that a herald may run with it.

For the revelation awaits an appointed time; it speaks of the end and will not prove false. Though it linger, wait for it; it will certainly come and will not delay.'[18]

This seems to be a great example for us to follow. It involves writing down what we know of the vision, honing it so it is simple and clear, sharing it with others to get their input and response, and then waiting. There is a time for the vision to be shared more publicly, but this early waiting period gives a chance to develop it as necessary. This is the waiting time. It is the time between vision and action. I believe that this is a key time for prayer. It is not down time. It is not wasted time. It is not drumming-fingers-on-tables time. It is prayer time. It is a time for patiently waiting before any observable action can take place. Don't get stuck in this place, but don't avoid it either. It is the place where the fire begins to catch and strengthen and grow hot!

3. Stoke the fire

You need to test the vision with people outside your immediate circle who might have some responsibility for implementing the vision over time – they need to be completely on board with it, understand it, recognise their place in it, and believe in it. Communicating the vision will be critically important.

This stage helps those who are hearing it to start thinking about how they fit into it themselves. This phase is where the intensity of the vision begins to grow when the church moves from listening to the vision to beginning to talk about it themselves. Invite people to talk about their own part in the vision – how they see it developing and what part they would like to play in it. This might include setting some measurable goals for the next two to five years and working out how they could see themselves making it happen. It's also a time to call people to pray and invest themselves in seeking God and calling on God to see the vision become a reality.

This sharing of the vision moves from top-down communication to a more viral form as leaders and then others catch the vision.

18 Habakkuk 2:2–3.

4. Spread the fire

The last stage of the vision-forming process is to write down the vision in a way that can be published for all to see. This means that new people joining in can quickly see what the vision is and catch it for themselves. Put it on banners and noticeboards and on your website. Talk about it regularly when you gather and encourage your leaders and teams to articulate the vision as they work it out in practice in their own areas of ministry.

In essence, keep communicating the vision so that it is affirmed and reaffirmed and everyone gets it. The leader might feel they're overdoing it, because they are constantly repeating it, but it takes a longer time than you think for the vision to be embedded in the church. It's worth thinking through how you can clearly and succinctly articulate your vision.

Three churches that I have been involved in from their conception express their vision in these terms:

- St Swithun's Bournemouth, also known as Lovechurch Bournemouth, says, 'as a community of people following Jesus, we want to be famous for love. We love God, love people, love life and that's why we Lovechurch.' They express this vision through evangelism and social action.

- Gas Street Church, Birmingham has a vision to be a 'Light for the City.' They say they 'need to be a church who gathers and scatters. We gather to worship and pray . . . to grow, to serve, to be family together. And then we scatter as compassionate followers of Jesus to be light-bearers, peace-makers, joy-bringers, and city-shapers wherever God sends us.'

- St Thomas, Newcastle has a simple three-fold vision, 'Following Jesus, Building Community, Loving Newcastle.' As an expression of this, they sent a missional community to build relationships in a deprived part of the city, and to serve it through youth work and community projects.

What is the God-shaped vision that he is sparking in you? How will you fan it into flame and stoke it into a fire that spreads and touches your whole community with the good news of Jesus?

VALUES

Vision is what we feel called to 'do:' values are how we choose to 'be' while carrying it out. Setting the values of a church plant is a vital part of laying strong foundations. Values are often not expressed verbally, but they are expressed in our behaviour and our actions, in what we choose to do and choose not to do. So thinking about values and articulating them from the outset will bring focus to what you are trying to do.

At St Paul's Shadwell, we had five values that emerged initially from conversations with my friend and colleague Miles Toulmin as we reflected on the values that we had experienced at HTB, our sending church. As I shared our chosen values with our church planting team, other leaders helped refine them further so that they were memorable, understandable, believable, theological, and visible. These were:

- **Audacity** – We wanted to 'Aim high,' expressing a desire to have audacious faith, and doing everything as well as we could.

- **Generosity** – We wanted to 'Give it away,' having a generous and missional mindset about giving the gospel away, as well as giving away leaders in time, to plant more churches.

- **Unity** – We wanted to 'Enjoy it together,' acknowledging that you have more fun in a team! We also wanted to work in unity with other churches because we could not do what God was calling us to do alone.

- **Humility** – We chose to 'Bow the knee,' recognising that we wanted to strive to maintain a posture of humility; worshipping God and honouring other leaders.

- **Tenacity** – We wanted to 'Never give up,' having a generational vision rather than something much shorter because we wanted our efforts to make a difference, leaving a legacy that would last beyond ourselves.

We found that these five values helped us think about how we wanted to go about making the vision happen. We wanted to do these things in a humble way, full of faith and boldness. We wanted to work alongside other people rather than alone, and to encourage a generosity of spirit and resources so that we could take the gospel to other places. We wanted to catalyse something that would have an impact on future generations and bring lasting transformation. Having these values on the tips of our tongues helped guide the way we thought and behaved, and they became something that we could hold up and measure against to see how we were doing.

Helen Shannon started church@five, a gathering on a Sunday afternoon in the Strawberry Vale Estate community centre in North London. The values of highly produced city centre resource churches differ from Helen's community. As she and the planting team were preparing to plant, the value that stood out at the centre of their vision was 'Come as you are.' In Helen's words, 'you don't need to dress up, you don't have to be a Christian, you don't have to have your life sorted . . . you can just come as you are.' Out of this central vision, four values emerged in her church:

1. **Bless** – The church wants to bless the estates they live on through service and love.
2. **Belong** – They want to welcome everyone to belong to their worshipping community, regardless of what stage of their journey of faith they are at.
3. **Believe** – The church is there to help people believe in Jesus.
4. **Become** – As part of this deepening of faith, the church is there to help people become more like Jesus through the presence and power of the Holy Spirit.

These foundational values helped Helen and her team as they planted church@five, giving them ways of understanding their ongoing approach. They were able to keep coming back to them, and they used them for teaching their church as they went forwards.

We also see the importance of clarifying values in rural church plants. Pete James planted St Basil's, a church based on a farm to the west of Exeter. He describes how the church's values have played a part in shaping their worshipping life:

> St Basil's has grown to become an ecosystem of people following the way of Jesus and seeking his renewal in the region. As we pursue this vision we hope to be characterised by four things – **God's Presence, Loving Community, Deep Formation, and Imaginative Mission** – which we call our Common Life. These values are kind of like a framework for life: priorities we seek to

organise our life around. Inspired by St Basil himself, we are doing all this distinctively in the rural environment, hoping to be beyond the city in a way that still blesses the city and prayerfully seeking a move of God right across this rural area we love to call home.

Red Lodge is part of the Lightwave Community in Suffolk. Diane Grano, its leader, talks about how the community's 'all hands to the pump' approach sees everyone included and valued in building community and journeying towards a personal relationship with God. Diane says that in her experience of this rural ministry, **collaboration, partnership, generosity** are key values. For example, if one of the Lightwave Community hubs is putting on an event, there is support from other hubs and also from local parish churches. Everyone comes together in unity. For both St Basil's and Red Lodge, their values help provide a framework for how they organise their worshipping life.

In a very different context, Richard Carter saw a need for monastic values in the centre of London. And so he started the Nazareth Community, a religious community which gathers members from many places, churches, and traditions, to 'seek God in contemplation, to acknowledge their dependence on God's grace, and to learn to live openly and generously with all.' The community is established on seven guiding principles: **Silence, Service, Scripture, Sacrament, Sharing, Sabbath Time, and Staying**. Members gather at St Martin's-in-the-Fields for eucharistic worship and contemplation. And as they disperse around the city, they embody these values in their everyday lives, as a prophetic response to its spiritual needs.

A VISION FOR ALL

As I have worked with church planters in our denomination and many others over the last 30 years, and especially now as a bishop where part of my calling is to work across the whole Church, I am convinced that God calls every part of the Church to be involved in this work of planting new churches. This will come in very different forms, using different names, different approaches, from different traditions of church, in different contexts, with different sizes of sending churches planting different sizes and shapes of new churches. To reach everyone with the gospel of Jesus Christ, and to communicate it in such a way that it is heard and understood, we need every Christian and every church and every denomination to be involved.

REVITALISATION

Church plants are not only planted from scratch. Many are revitalisations of old churches (sometimes called grafts) where a need for something new has been discerned. Your vision might pick up something of the past that has faded. The apostle John tells us, 'unless a grain of wheat falls to the ground and dies, it remains only a single seed. But if it dies, it produces many seeds.'[19] God may have given you a vision to bring new life, either to an existing church with a declining congregation or one that has been closed altogether.

I believe that revitalising an old church involves similar practices to planting a new church. It will require new or renewed vision, new leadership and an incoming team. But there is the added challenge of integrating old and new, often with a fresh mandate for change. The incoming team will need to be compassionate and sensitive to those who have been long term members of an existing congregation who may in turn be grieving the loss of the church as it was. Equally, the existing congregation will require encouragement and support to welcome the new people coming to join them. There will need to be an intentional process of unifying the two groups together in a united vision, or re-vision, for what lies ahead.

A revitalisation doesn't end there. It might go on to carry out further planting itself within its own area or parish, or even go on to revitalise other churches, as happened in my own experience.

I suspect that in the coming years the Church of England, and other denominations and networks, will need more and more revitalisations to take place so this subject probably deserves a book of its own.

YOUR VISION

No matter what people group you are trying to reach, or church tradition you inhabit, or missional approach you want to use, there is a need, with a posture of humility, to embody and embrace a vision that captures your heart, that is shaped around who God has shaped you to be, with your gifts and passions, that is right for your context, arising from what God is and has been doing around you, and that is founded in the purposes of God. In that sense it is deeply personal because you will live it out with others.

19 John 12:24.

As you articulate your vision to others, it can be caught and developed by those who are with you, and becomes compelling for all who encounter it. And it will be founded on values that move people to say, I want to be part of that too. With this intertwined foundation of vision and prayer, we can move on to some of the practical details of planning, understanding the context we are going to, growing a team, and resourcing the church plant effectively.

CALL TO ACTION: VISION

The first task on the Plant Course is to articulate your church plant's vision using an 'elevator pitch.' Imagine being in a lift or elevator with a potential team member or intercessor or financial supporter who might help you. You've got 30 seconds to make your pitch. What will you say? How will you phrase it? It is good practice for leaders to create and hone their pitch into three to four sentences that are compelling, informative, and memorable. I have found it takes many iterations to get it right but it is worth it. It helps you clarify what you are doing and why, as well as helping others catch that vision and join in too.

Here's a possible framework to start to hone your vision:

- What's the need?
- What's the opportunity?
- What are you going to do about it?
- What difference will it make?
- How can others be involved?

3

PLANNING

HOW TO PREPARE FOR YOUR PLANT

Everyone knows it's important to plan, but many of us don't actually do it, or do it sufficiently, perhaps because we don't know where to start.

The first thing to understand is that we are in the hands of the Lord. There is the encouragement to plan: 'Commit to the Lord whatever you do, and he will establish your plans.'[1] Intriguingly, there is also the sense that the outcomes are out of our hands: 'Many are the plans in a person's heart, but it is the Lord's purpose that prevails.'[2] It seems to me that we are to embrace both insights together – to plan well, doing all we can using our God-given minds and talents, entrusting them to the Lord, and to trust the outcome to him.

The writer of Proverbs tells us more. It is wise to get advice: 'Plans are established by seeking advice,'[3] and 'Plans fail for lack of counsel, but with many advisors they succeed.'[4] I strongly encourage anyone following a call to plant a church to get training – join a training course like the Plant Course – as well as working with a team to multiply the wisdom using the different gifts and insights from each person as you plan together. Also, planning is not just a cerebral exercise but something that draws on passion and the heart: 'May he give you the desire of your heart and make all your plans succeed.'[5] We are planning for something that will change people's lives as they come to know the love and saving power of Jesus Christ in their lives. Church planting is truly transformational.

In the life of Jesus, we can see that he had a clear plan and strategy. His mission involved training up 12 people who he sent out in twos. In a

1 Proverbs 16:3.
2 Proverbs 19:21.
3 Proverbs 20:18.
4 Proverbs 15:22.
5 Psalm 20:4.

second phase, he sends out the 72 to the towns around Galilee.[6] Jesus gave them specific instructions, asking them for feedback upon their return, to which he gave a response. We can see how the early church grew out of this intention. Jesus was strategic and he had a plan; his goals were clear. He even clarified what he was not going to do.[7]

When it comes to church planting there is so much to do, involving great expense of time, energy, and resources. I believe it is vital to make a plan, so that you can focus and anticipate as much as possible. Then, even if the plan has to change (which it will!), nothing is wasted – the planning time and energy you have put in will make you more agile and able to respond to changing situations.

However, I know there are some who baulk at the idea of making a plan. They would prefer to say, 'The plan is to have no plan.' Similarly, when the word strategy is used, it seems to switch people off, as if making plans and having a strategy take God's matters into our hands too much. I believe the psalmist, the writer of Proverbs, and Jesus tell an alternative story, along with anyone in history who has seen great fruit from careful planning and implementation. Planning is vital to the overall process of preparing for a church plant, as all the various elements of what might be involved are brought together, and from this early planning, a clear strategy can now emerge.

While the first two chapters of this book were about foundations, this chapter is about putting scaffolding around the emerging structure. Planning always needs to be careful and systematic and it is worth putting in the time to do this well. We'll look at practical things like timings, priorities, and communication along with important ecclesiological aspects including planning for evangelism and discipleship. I believe that planning is best done in a learning environment with your team.

CHURCH PLANTING TRAINING

Most church planters I know are get-on-with-it types who are highly creative and entrepreneurial and the thought of having to do extra training usually turns them off. However, they would still benefit greatly from training! They will be made to consider all sorts of eventualities, gain

6 Luke 10.
7 Matthew 15:24.

a wider perspective, and realise how much there is to learn from others, immediately cutting across any arrogance and the pride that comes before a fall.

When I started out, there were no training courses on church planting in the Anglican Church. The Vineyard had developed some training and I got hold of their excellent training manual, written by Steve Nicholson. After reading his training manual I bought up all their remaining stock to give to friends asking for training materials because it was so helpful to me. Bob and Mary Hopkins, who ran Anglican Church Planting Initiatives, had lots of advice and had written up case studies of various kinds. However, I gathered most from simply sitting over coffee with previous planters in our small church network.

I would now say that training is essential, especially if it is orientated around preparing for the actual plant you are doing. Training can fall into two categories – learning about church planting in general, and learning how to do it in practice. I have found that people ask different questions depending on their situation. If it is general learning, questions are more esoteric and theoretical, and sometimes combative. When someone is preparing for a church plant themselves, questions are practical and, in some cases, desperate! We developed our training at the Gregory Centre for the latter and I have likened it to SAS training – they do it with live ammunition: it's a real situation and it has to help you right away.

The Gregory Centre has developed several training resources to provide for the needs of different planting pathways. The Plant Course is specifically designed for church planters who have a defined timescale to the launch of their new church plant and a team identified. Alongside this we have established Myriad for lay planters whose vision and team will emerge over a longer period of time. Become, a course which trains emerging leaders from low income housing estates has also been created. And, in partnership with others, CCX has created London Pioneer School, which trains pioneers to establish new worshipping communities. All foster a learning environment in community with other planters so that each one can learn, not just for their own context, but also learning from difference, as there is almost always huge variety between what each planter is doing in practice. There is no one single model of planting, but we ask questions that can be applied to any approach, and we draw on hundreds of examples of church plants as they plan. We encourage planters to come with a team so that learning is more corporate and decisions can be made together, rather than needing to do it away from the group. For any context, these are the questions that I ask.

I can't encourage you strongly enough to invest in training. The eternal destiny of the people who will come to faith in your plant is the motivation to do the most we can, in the best way we can, in the short time we have. We owe it to them to do the best planning possible. If you don't have access to your own training, sign up for the Plant Course or other learning pathways at the Gregory Centre. You won't regret it![8]

STRATEGY

The main reason we need to plan for church planting is to think through what we are trying to do and how we are going to get there. This is a simple way of describing what strategy is. We see it throughout Scripture. When God told Nehemiah to rebuild Jerusalem's walls, he worked out a well thought through strategy to accomplish it. Joseph planned ahead to save Egypt from famine. David worked out a plan to bring the resources necessary to help his son, Solomon, build the Temple. The apostle Paul developed his strategic approach with each missionary journey.

One of my chief aims in writing this book is to help you to plan well. I am drawing on the wisdom and experiences of the many hundreds of church plants we have supported and been involved with in England and in other parts of the world. For this, we like to use a 'Leader's Map'[9] to start to work out the strategy for each plant.

The idea behind a Leader's Map is to clarify on a single page the journey you need to go on from where you are now to the vision that describes where you want to get to. The journey is rarely a straight line because there may be opportunities that might take you on a slightly different route, as well as risks that push you off course. The values you live by will help you stay on track towards goals that will help you measure your progress, as you work out the first steps you need to take. By putting them on a single page, it helps you and your team to know where you are at any

8 At the time of writing, St Hild College offers a Church Planting track for Anglican ordinands and Baptist ministers-in-training, and Seedbed, a year-long training for lay planters.
9 Andy Blacknell, who developed the Plant Course with me, has written more on this idea in his book, *LEAD*, co-written with Andy Coombs and John Greenway.

particular stage and helps you not get distracted from what you are trying to achieve. I have used this tool in various ways for many years in our own church planting and also for working through changes in ministry that need focus, direction, and resolve.

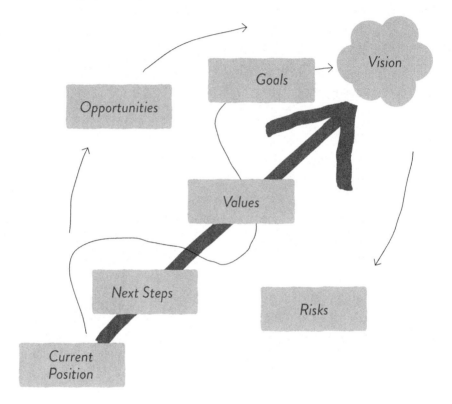

Figure 2: The Leader's Map

To clarify the big picture direction and strategy of your church plant, address questions in these seven areas:

1. **Vision** – What is your big aspiration? What is the picture of a better future that your church plant will enable? This is the vision part we spoke about in chapter 2. This needs to be a simple and clear statement of what you are hoping to achieve over time. Over the weeks of planning, this will need to be sharpened and honed so everyone understands what it is and why you're doing it.

2. **Values** – How will you go about achieving it? What are the values that will underpin your church plant? What are your 'golden rules?' This was covered in chapter 2 too. It is how you are going to achieve the vision through your behaviours and practices, expressed in a succinct, attractive, and memorable way. Having your values on the tip of your tongue will help guide the way you think and act, and so we encourage people to think these things through, and to make them fresh and easy to remember and pass on.

3. **Goals** – What are the measurable signs that will show you if you have succeeded in what you are trying to do? This will involve turning the vision into something that can be tracked and counted so you know how you are doing and when you have achieved what you were aiming for. If you have a goal of getting 100 people to come along to your church within three months, you are going to do things very differently than if your goal was to build a small community, gathering 30 people over two years. Establishing your goals will help you measure how you are going to go about it, what you are aiming for, and let you know if you are achieving it. Your goals should be: specific, measurable, achievable, realistic, and time-bound (SMART). It is helpful to pin these goals down, and to work out if you have achieved what you set out to do! If you have, then you can celebrate those things. If not, you can ask why.

   For example, the London Diocese set a goal of planting or renewing 100 new worshipping communities by 2020 as part of their Capital Vision 2020 programme and this helped focus some of their resources, training, and energy in order to achieve the goal. They got to 87 just before the Covid-19 pandemic changed their pace, achieving their goal a year later. By setting this goal over seven years, they also increased their rate of planting by a factor of six compared to the previous 28 years. Goal-setting and measurement helps to evaluate and fine-tune your efforts.

4. **Current position** – Where are you on the journey of your plant? Nationally, the Church of England has 1.6 per cent of the population attending one of its churches regularly. Locally, that

number might be more or less, but it still leaves a lot of people to proclaim the gospel to! Where are you in terms of building a team? What is your relationship with the diocese or other oversight body? Where are you with the timings? How ready are you? These are all aspects that might be considered as you look at this part of the map.

5. **Opportunities** – What might help advance your progress towards your vision? This might include buildings – which can be a blessing or a burden! The parish in Shadwell that we planted into had fantastic buildings that could accommodate different groups and offices, but it also came with a Grade II* listing and a ceiling repair bill of £70,000 on day one. You might have people on your team who bring particular gifts and skills that will make a huge difference. A church in Hounslow wanting to plant in their area had a Gujarati and Hindi-speaking leader who had planted many, many churches in India. He was an essential asset on the team in bringing the good news of Jesus to the people around them.

6. **Risks** – What might hinder or stop you from achieving your vision? This is the flip side of opportunities. This might include opposition from groups of people. A church revitalisation, merging an incoming planting team with an existing dwindling congregation, is almost always a great blessing but it can involve fear of the unknown and of change that needs to be handled with sensitivity and care. Local churches can feel threatened by a new church plant so this is a risk, but equally they can be an opportunity to get to know the local area well and be introduced to other community stakeholders. Finances might be part of your risk list if you do not have enough for the medium term. Some church plants, like rockets, need large amounts of energy to get them launched, and the funds to get them started need to be matched with funding to sustain them. Resources should be considered carefully, and we'll go into this in greater depth in chapter 8.

When we were preparing to plant two churches out of St Paul's Shadwell, one person very generously offered a large proportion of the necessary financial resources. They promised to give £50,000 towards a church plant in Bow, and another £50,000 to a church plant going to Bethnal Green. On that basis, we took this as a green light to go for it and plant. Some months later, within weeks of launching the plants, we called to follow up on the offer, only to discover that the person who had promised the money couldn't be found anywhere. We were faced with the huge challenge of finding £100,000 for something that we were already committed to. This trial led to huge generosity, and we raised £85,000 within a short amount of time, largely because of one generous donor who encouraged others to give too. It is good to go in with your eyes open, aware of the biggest risks, whether they be people or resources, that might hold you back. Any number of things can happen, and it's important to make plans on the basis of things changing quickly, or not going so well.

7. **Next steps** – What are the next steps you need to take to achieve your vision? This will involve working through your mid-term priorities and working out who does what, when. How will you gather a team? How will you develop discipleship and evangelism? How much money will it cost – at the beginning and for the first few years? What needs to be focused on in the first year and second year? When will you plant again? We use additional tools to help work these questions through – timelines, priority planning, stakeholder engagement, budgets, etc. But for now, keep it high level in your thinking.

In summary, start addressing these questions to help you develop your strategy:

1. **Vision** – What is your big picture dream?
2. **Values** – What are your values that will underpin the plant?
3. **Goals** – What will success look like? How will you know?
4. **Current position** – Where are you on the journey?
5. **Opportunities** – What will help you progress?
6. **Risks** – What may hold you back?
7. **Next steps** – What are your mid-term priorities?

You will need to keep coming back to your strategic plan as situations change!

TIMELINE TOOLS

The next thing to consider is what you do when, from the moment of conception to the first few years after planting. I have learned from many mistakes of getting the timing wrong, whether it is doing too much at once or not doing things in the right order. There are important steps to follow in launching and developing a church plant. Some of them are consecutive; some of them happen concurrently. I have found that a helpful way to think this through is by using a timeline. This is simply a calendar, drawn along a line, which allows you to anticipate the steps involved in church planting.

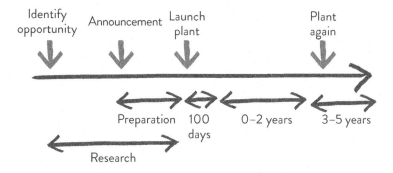

Figure 3: A linear timeline

Here are some typical steps along the timeline that are important to think through:

Identify the opportunity

This might involve the identification of a planter, a place, and permission to proceed. In the Church of England, if you plant inside your parish, that involves the senior church leader (incumbent) and the Parish Church Council (PCC); if it is outside your parish, it requires a bishop to affirm this, which might include working with a deanery, a diocesan or Area council in order to get all parties to be aware, understanding, and, if necessary, agreed on what is happening. On average, this might be a year before launching a plant.

Working out where to plant is often a decision between several parties. If it is a revitalisation, the bishop, archdeacon, and area dean might suggest places they think could be revitalised over time; while the sending church might identify places it feels it could plant to over a similar period. The places that overlap provide a starting point for exploration together. With prayer and good communication, the right places emerge at the right times, and this requires much grace and much trust. Careful communication with the various stakeholders is essential and must be planned well.

As we will discuss later, it is also important for the church planter to agree with their sending church leader the process of planting and what resources might be expected from the sending church. One critical conversation, for example, needs to consider who might be approached to join the team. If there is a key leader and significant giver who is either invited or has expressed interest in joining the planting team, a conversation with the senior leader would be important as that person would leave a big hole in terms of essential skills and church income. That might be the right decision but this can be planned well in terms of training others to replace them and encouraging others to give in order to replace that funding. It might be wise to have regular planning meetings between sender and planter to discuss preparation and progress where these kinds of questions can be on the agenda.

Announcement

This happens generally about six months pre-launch. This is done to make sure everyone is aware of the plant and to begin to start inviting people to pray and think through joining the team. It is also a season of sharing the embryonic vision of what you are proposing to do, listening to people's responses, and allowing the vision to adapt as others share insights and stories that enhance and bring colour to it.

Once you announce your plant, there is no going back, and so you have to ensure that it is done well. Part of this is making sure that everyone who needs to know is told, and doing that in the right order. Some people need to know before it's announced, so they get to hear about it from you and not someone else. When we announced that we were planting from HTB to St Paul's Shadwell, we had planned to announce it simultaneously at both churches. The first HTB service was at 8 a.m., and the St Paul's Shadwell service was at 9:30 a.m. In that brief window of time, news of the plant had made its way to St Paul's Shadwell, before the archdeacon managed to make the official announcement there! This caused some upset, so as a lesson to others, be aware of how to announce the plant, and try as much as possible to anticipate some upset and take steps to alleviate it where possible.

Preparation

Four essential elements should be considered as you prepare for planting.

1. **Prayer** – First is laying a strong and sure foundation of prayer, as outlined in chapter 1. This is the absolute essential investment we can ever make in the work of church planting. The invitation from God in the Scriptures is to pray relentlessly: 'Devote yourselves to prayer, being watchful and thankful.'[10] 'Rejoice always, pray continually, give thanks in all circumstances; for this is God's will for you in Christ Jesus.'[11] 'This is the confidence we have in approaching God: that if we ask anything according to his will, he hears us.'[12] This leads me to get excited about praying because it is so powerful and transformative in terms of God's provision, guidance, and equipping for all that lies ahead. Plan for prayer and set aside time for it, personally and corporately. Do all you can to get it on other people's prayer agendas. The more prayer the better!

2. **Preparing yourself** – The second element is preparing yourself, through prayer, through research, through training and seeking advice. When I planted there were only two people I went to because there weren't many people who had revitalised churches at that stage. I had coffee with them and drilled them for answers to my many questions. The one piece of advice I remember most of all was about pacing yourself and not trying to do everything all at once. I am afraid I promptly forgot that and our plant was too busy too soon, leading to my exhaustion. Much of this chapter is about ensuring planters don't repeat the mistakes I made!

10 Colossians 4:2.
11 1 Thessalonians 5:16–18.
12 1 John 5:14.

3. **Casting the vision** – Thirdly, preparation involves casting the vision for the plant in earnest and inviting people to join you. We held fortnightly open meetings on Sunday afternoons at our sending church to share the vision, highlight opportunities to serve, hear from local people about the area and its needs, and pray together. We offered the opportunity for people to sign up for weekly newsletters to stay in touch and we suggested different ways people could get involved – praying, supporting with skills or gifts, giving financially, or joining the team. Sandy Millar, my sending church leader, suggested encouraging people to commit for one year to join the team. For it to become viable, it would need people to stay much longer than that, but in London, especially as a young person, a year feels like a long time. For them, it was a big commitment but also one that felt doable. This gives a new plant momentum and energy. Many who come will stay on, and they need to be people who will commit to being a full part of the church community, praying, giving financially, and helping to disciple others. When the team is generous, this creates a culture of generosity. New disciples come into the church and see serving and financial giving as something that is normal. When each of the team commits to discipling someone else – encouraging people to follow Jesus in and through their lives – we will make disciples who make other disciples.

    Sometimes members of the team come from another church. If that is the case, we should encourage them to go to their church leader to ask if they are happy with this move. In some cases, it might be better for these individuals to remain at their current church. They might be people who would distract from the vision. Equally, a church might suffer heavy losses if particular individuals were to leave, in which case a discussion is necessary as to whether they join the team later, giving them time to replace themselves by training someone else up. It's important to think about the individuals on your team, and where they are coming from.

    One month before the launch, you might consider making a final call for a commitment, asking people if they are 'in.' You can't force people to stay, but this gives a sense of being on an adventure together and committing with each other to love and serve in a deeper way. You might like to consider how you prepare the whole for what lies ahead.

4. **Practical matters** – Fourthly, there are many personal and practical things to get in place too during this phase – for us it involved moving house, changing schools for our children, finishing ministry responsibilities, and training others in the sending church where I had worked for 13 years, as well as planning the launch and first days, weeks, and months of what lay ahead. It's not unlike any church move, but looking after a team and thinking through the change issues adds extra pressure that planning can alleviate.

Launch

It is important to think through how the church plant begins. There are at least a couple of options here. One is a 'big bang' launch, with lots of publicity leading up to a launch event with lots of momentum. The opposite of this is the 'slow burn,' where you start small with a few people, and grow slowly. These might start in homes, and as the group grows, the groups begin to multiply and gather in a number of homes. Eventually, these groups might gather together and form one larger group. This is a slower, but deeper, way of forming a church. Whether you launch with a bang or grow slowly depends on your context and situation. Either way, it is helpful to have a date of 'launch' to aim for as you plan. We'll come back to this in chapter 9.

The first 100 days

When something is new, it is important to build trust and momentum, and to be as organised as possible. It is also likely that you will face unexpected challenges that can absorb a lot of extra time. Thinking through the first 100 days of your plant, post launch, helps you plan as much as possible to cover the unexpected. So build in a rhythm of staff meetings, church gatherings, prayer times, days off, meetings with local leaders and other churches. Give time for administrative business, but also mission, evangelism, and prayer-walking. Seeing it all on one page gives a feel for what you need to prioritise.

The first two years

In the first year, everything is new and being done for the first time. It is demanding because everything needs thinking through, contextualising, planning, and constantly reviewing. The second year is similar, because inevitably you find ways of improving what you did the first time round. By the third year, you will have established your rhythm and settled down. I remember feeling so deflated in August as our numbers went down quickly. They clawed back in September. It happened again but even more the following year. I wondered whether what we were doing was sustainable. Sure enough, when September came round, people returned and more joined the church. It was of course the holiday season, but I realised that the people who had joined the church did actually want to come back after their holidays! After that, we were not as concerned each summer, and we deliberately reduced activity to give ourselves more of a rest too.

The temptation in a new plant is to start everything at once, to establish mature practices and ministries because that is often what you have experienced in your sending church. There might even be demand for certain ministries or offers from new members to help start them. If you try to do everything all at once it is unlikely you will be able to do it all as well as you would like. You won't have established teams, well thought through practices, or even sufficient awareness of whether there is a need for that particular ministry. We made that mistake and we got exhausted, and the church felt tired too. We needed to review what was needed and when was the best time to deliver it. I now encourage teams to spread out the starting of new ministries across that first two-year period. You might think about your first two years as six termly blocks (see figure 4).

Then begin to work out with your team what you want to introduce. Resisting the temptation, and even the demand, to start everything in term 1, work out what could be delayed. Term 1 is about beginning to gather, and might include a new Sunday service. It might include a central prayer gathering. You might start an evangelistic course that term too or leave it to term 2, once the team has got to know people in the area and relationships are strong enough to invite them to a course. Midweek groups might start later, following the evangelistic course, as well as giving appropriate time to train leaders for the discipleship and pastoral care involved in them. Adding community outreach and mission, leadership development, and other events and courses may be done as required. This approach helps reach a balance in your activity, increases the quality of what you are doing, and ensures the team doesn't burn out. Additionally, this approach helps communicate to others that a particular activity is in the plan, and it also gives a way of swapping new activities around if they need to be done earlier or can wait later.

	Term 1: Sep–Dec	Term 2: Jan–Apr	Term 3: May–Aug
Year 1	Sunday Service Alpha	Small groups Leadership training	Social transformation ministry
Year 2	Additional service Family life course	Lent course	Holiday club

Figure 4: An example of the first two years. Don't start everything at once!

Years 3–5

Within five years you should have established rhythms and relationships and have a strong sense of identity. A five-year plan can be much looser, but will encompass your big goals. For example, within five years you might like to plant another church, be a certain size, have more than one congregation, to have made a measurable impact on your community, or to have seen a particular number of baptisms. Write these goals down, share them with others, pray for them and plan for them. In my experience, newly planted churches that have *not* planted within five years are unlikely to plant at all. Plan to plant again from the beginning.

Sandy Millar always used to say that we often overestimate what can be done in the first year, and underestimate what can be done in five years. It is both an encouragement to be patient in the short term and ambitious in the longer term.

Pulling all this together can be shown by way of a linear timeline, as in figure 4, or shown as a Gantt chart, like the one here, which helps show what can be done concurrently, as well as what phases are dependent on others before they can be started.

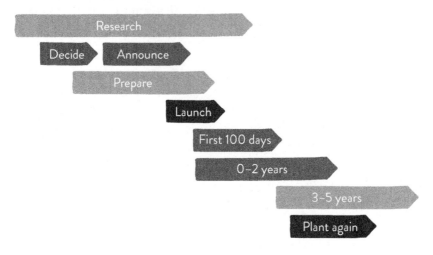

Figure 5: The stages of a church plant in Gantt chart format, showing the dependencies and concurrence of particular phases

The Fresh Expressions journey is a little different, with less certain timings and outcomes. Nevertheless, having clear goals and good communication as to what the emerging church is doing helps us to better understand the journey of church development over time. These are the stages of the Fresh Expressions journey, with the last three steps being critical to the formation of a church and its reproduction and multiplication:

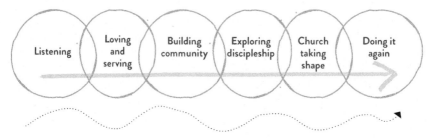

Underpinned by prayer, ongoing listening, and relationship with the wider church

Figure 6: The Fresh Expressions pathway

STAKEHOLDERS

Many people have a part to play in making church plants happen. Sometimes they have a decisive part. It is helpful to identify these people and establish what role they might have and how they might impact, positively or negatively, the outcomes of what you are trying to achieve. These 'stakeholders' are individuals or groups who have a particular interest in the plant. There are four ways they might impact the plant: making it happen in a decisive way; helping it move forwards in some way; letting it happen in the sense of not standing in its way; or stopping it from happening (decisive in a negative sense). Identifying and then working out how to engage with each of these people or groups becomes critically important for the success of what you are trying to do. Here is another way of looking at it[13]:

Barriers   Bystanders   Advocates   Champions

Figure 7: Stakeholder identification: what role might they be playing?

I think that the story of Elymas in Acts 13:6–12 illustrates this. The proconsul and leading governor of Cyprus was called Sergius Paulus. He sent for Paul and Barnabas because he was interested in hearing the word of the Lord. Elymas, a local sorcerer, tried to turn the proconsul away from hearing from them. Paul pronounced God's judgement on Elymas such that he went blind for a time and the proconsul was amazed about the teaching of the Lord. Elymas was stopping the gospel from being heard and was trying to make the proconsul stop them too. Paul needed to engage both of them to enable the outcome to be more favourable. May our stakeholders be more like the proconsul!

13 Andy Blacknell, who developed the Plant Course with me, produced this diagram and has written more on this idea in his book, *LEAD*, co-written with Andy Coombs and John Greenway.

The planning task here is to identify everyone who has a part to play in the church plant, then to identify what role they have to play, how they might move to being more helpful, and what kind of engagement they need in terms of communication. Here are some typical stakeholders:

Local residents
Local influencers
The local council
Venue owners
Local church leaders
Local newspapers
Bishop/overseer
Archdeacon
Area Dean
Local clergy
Bishop's council
Finance committee
Sending church leader
Sending church supporters
Sending church staff
Intercession team
Church network
Funders

What role might each of your stakeholders be playing? Are they 'barriers', perhaps not allowing parking next to the church? Can you move them to being 'bystanders' who let the church plant have parking, or perhaps even becoming 'advocates', helping it as they are touched by the interactions? Or are the people 'champions' who are vital to the success of the whole adventure? Whoever they are, it is important to work out what role they are playing, where you want them to be, how you will engage with them – a meeting, a phone call, an email, or a flyer – and when you need to do it – now, or once the plant is at a particular stage.

There are two tools you might find helpful for this. Firstly, the stakeholder mapping tool which helps plot where each person might be in terms of whether they are of high importance to success and how committed they are. Names can be inserted in each quadrant.

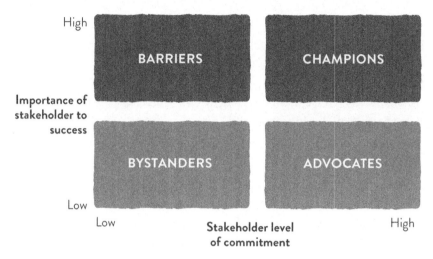

Figure 9: Stakeholder mapping tool: where is each stakeholder?

The second tool brings all this together as a stakeholder action chart. Who is going to engage with the person or group, when, and how, and what is the desired outcome of your engagement with them? Use this to help you work out your next steps.

Stakeholder	Who	Current position	Desired position	Priority	Action	When
		Stop it/Let it/Help it/Make it		Low/Medium/High		
1						
2						
3						
4						

Figure 10: Stakeholder action chart: what do you need to do?

EVANGELISM AND DISCIPLESHIP PLANS

In the end, church planting is all about making disciples who follow Jesus, live their lives in his kingdom, and pass on their faith to others. This is perhaps the most important part of your planning and it will continually evolve as you spend more time understanding your context and the people within it. So how do you plan for disciple-making? After all, we usually inherit a discipleship strategy in the churches we attend, whether it has been thought through or not!

A good place to start with this is the practice of the early church in Acts 2:42–7:

> They devoted themselves to the apostles' teaching and to fellowship, to the breaking of bread and to prayer. Everyone was filled with awe at the many wonders and signs performed by the apostles. All the believers were together and had everything in common. They sold property and possessions to give to anyone who had need. Every day they continued to meet together in the temple courts. They broke bread in their homes and ate together with glad and sincere hearts, praising God and enjoying the favour of all the people. And the Lord added to their number daily those who were being saved.

Here we see the early disciples focusing on the apostles' teaching, fellowship, eating together, and praying together. This includes giving to the church and sharing lives and possessions with one another, worshipping together in a gathered community (temple courts) and in homes. Systematically, we can think through how disciples will grow in their faith corporately, in smaller groups (homes), and individually. Thom Rainer and Eric Geiger's research shows that growth happens most commonly in churches where there is a simple structure that is understandable to everyone.[14] What might a simple and understandable structure be for anyone who comes to your church plant?

To draw in new disciples, you need to find ways for them to hear the gospel of Jesus Christ and join your church. What is your evangelism plan? How can you make the most of specific opportunities to talk about Jesus or to invite people to encounter the love of God? Here are some starting points for thinking this through.

---

14 See Thom Rainer and Eric Geiger, *Simple Church* (Nashville, TN: B&H Publishing, 2011).

Personal invitations

The evangelist Billy Graham said people need about 26 separate encounters and invitations to church before they are ready to become a Christian. Vineyard church leader Steve Nicholson, who has taught and researched church planting as well as doing it himself many times, says that the first 50 people who come to your plant are most likely to have been personally invited by the plant leader. He also says the next 50 who join the church are most likely to have been invited by the plant leader too, though the plant leader is also now looking after the first 50 as their pastor. Encouragingly, he has found that the next 50 to come are most likely to have been invited by existing church members as they now have the confidence to invite others, having seen their plant leader doing it. This is describing the growth of medium to larger churches, but the principle of the leader taking a lead in getting to know and inviting others stays true. Leaders especially should be intentional about making time in their diaries to invite others – neighbours, shopkeepers, other people they encounter in their everyday lives. Over time, that will set a whole culture of invitation so it becomes normal for others to do the same.

Natural evangelists

I have found that there are about 10 per cent of our congregations who are naturally good at talking about Jesus to their friends and families or who find it easy to invite them to church. Find out who these connectors are and encourage them in particular to keep inviting people. At the same time, pray for more connectors in your congregation.

Prayer

Plan for praying for the church to grow. Be creative about praying for non-Christian friends and neighbours. Do prayer-walks (see chapter 1). Join in with the Thy Kingdom Come movement[15] that encourages prayer for five people to come to know Jesus during the 10 days before Pentecost. As with all these ideas, build them into your preparation time and your first 100 days to set it as part of your church culture.

---

15 https://www.thykingdomcome.global/.

Leafleting

Letting local people know your church is up and running, as well as inviting them to specific events like Christmas services, etc.

Door-knocking

Along with leafleting, get to know people by meeting them on their own turf. Giving a gift or doing a survey or simply introducing yourself is a powerful way of expressing love and care. In Shadwell, we lived on a very busy four-lane highway but we had 20 to 30 houses either side of us on our side of the road. Louie and I invited them all, twice a year – at Christmas and in the summer – to come to our home and experience hospitality; we had parties of all kinds to try to connect with the different people who were our neighbours. I soon learned that there was only one grumpy person who didn't like being invited. Everyone else was very grateful and many of them came. In time, two of them came to church and became Christians and are still following the Lord today. We just built that into our annual rhythm as a family.

Christmas services

Don't just do one special service. The evangelist J John says think about it like ice cream flavours – people like different flavours – so apply it to Christmas. Have different ways of encountering the message of Christmas, whether it is traditional carols, informal carols, children's crib services, school carol services in your church, beer and carols in the local pub, etc.

Signage

Can your church be found? Work with the local council to have signage on streets so people can find you! If you own your building, your grounds provide the greatest advertising space going – and it is totally in your hands as to how you use it.

Website

This is the most popular way people will find out about your church. Ensure it is up to date and aimed as much at the newcomer as it is for existing members. Look at it from the view of someone who has never been to church before and make it accessible for them.

Guest services

Have a variety of approaches to help attract new people and make them feel welcome, perhaps with guest speakers, Back-to-Church Sundays, Mother's Day and Father's Day services, etc. The Church calendar is powerful when it is used as an evangelistic tool – Advent, Christmas, Epiphany, Ash Wednesday, Lent, Easter, Ascension, Pentecost, All Saints; with creativity they can all become evangelistic opportunities to invite others. St Katharine Cree hosts a new church for hidden workers in the City of London. They began by holding a carol service for cleaners one Christmas. That service gave them proper recognition for their work, mostly unseen and out of hours, and created community within a service of worship. Now they meet monthly and are growing as they invite colleagues and friends to join them.

Altar calls

Get into the habit of offering opportunities for people to become Christians at church gatherings, whether Sunday services, midweek groups, courses, or events. When this is done in a confident but low-key way, it becomes a normal part of who you are as a church. Again, churches that are intentional about this have more people becoming new Christians.

Alpha

I have found that churches that are intentional about evangelism are generally better at it than churches that are not. One obvious way is to host an evangelistic course like Alpha, Exploring Faith, and Christianity Explored on an ongoing basis so that there is always a course for new people to join.

Courses

If you offer courses like marriage preparation or debt advice, ensure that guests hear about the church, and help them with the next step if they want to find out more.

An evangelistic culture

I have been hugely influenced by the late Tim Keller, former author, pastor, and founder of the City to City church planting movement. He said that if you preach as if half the congregation were not Christians, appealing to their mindset, needs, and lifestyle, then over time, you will attract non-Christians in increasing numbers. In his church, he set an evangelistic and invitational culture in a very intentional way. You can do this through preaching programmes, content, and a welcoming environment. Put it in the plan!

As you engage with people, how will you develop discipleship more generally as they grow in their faith? You could invent your own process, but there is so much to do in preparing and starting up a new Christian community that I recommend you consider using something 'off the shelf' and adapting it to your context. This might include introduction to faith courses like the Alpha course, Christianity Explored, and Exploring Faith, or Bible study groups with the huge number of resources aimed at supporting small group discipleship. You might choose to invite people to a course that aims to help those invited and experience it in a Christian context. At St Paul's Shadwell, we offered The Marriage Course several times and we consistently had a third of guests from our own community, a third from other churches, and a third from outside the church altogether. The local mosque sent couples to us because they said it was the best place locally to have support in this area of life.

There is no one right way of enabling evangelism and discipleship pathways in your plant, but if it is to happen, you must put time into thinking, praying, and structuring church activity and messaging so that people understand it and know how to engage with it.

SOCIAL JUSTICE PLANS

God doesn't just love those who follow him. He loves and delights in every person who has ever lived and will ever live. As the Church, we are his representatives here on earth; we are here to spread the good news and to be a channel of his love in the world. For this reason, every church and every church plant should be involved in feeding the hungry, giving drink to the thirsty, welcoming the stranger, clothing the naked, caring for the sick, and visiting those in prison.[16]

There are a number of things you can do as a plant. It might be the case that you put on initiatives where your church can offer a service to people on the margins in your community: a food bank, warm banks, ESOL classes, support groups for sex workers, debt support and advice, free meals for the community. You might want to offer your space for an Alcoholics or Narcotics Anonymous group to rent from you. Other plants use times of worship to speak into broader injustices in society. A powerful approach is found in those churches who build up the agency of people they're trying to help, through training in community organising, leadership, and other skills, so that they can become the agents of change in their lives and communities. Clarity for discerning what you do emerges from researching your particular context. I'll cover that in the next chapter.

Whatever you choose to do, it is important to make sure that response to human suffering is part of the DNA of your plant. Vision is key here. Sometimes plants make this explicit in their vision; for example, social justice is one of the 'Four Elements' at the heart of Choir Church, and St Katharine Cree is a church in London for hidden workers. Other plants include social justice implicitly in their vision. For example, Harbour Church, Portsmouth, along with many other HTB network churches, state that, 'We want to play our part in the evangelisation of the nation, the revitalisation of the church and the transformation of society.' Out of this vision comes their food bank, support for sex workers, debt support, and community meals. Sermons and other parts of worship services can be used to address injustice and prioritise social justice.

My hope is that through revealing God's love to your communities, people will come to love him. Time and time again, I have seen how social justice becomes a credible foundation for evangelism. Fr Ross Gunderson, the vicar of St Etheldreda's, Fulham set up a charity to feed people during the pandemic. He says:

> The result was that even though some parishes were shrinking, we began to grow. We fed 5,000 people a week with the help of volunteers; people who never came to church started to see St Eth's as their home and wanted to help.

16 Matthew 25:35–40.

We bought stuff people needed and delivered it and we set up a hotline for people to call. We had daily reflections on social media. We wanted to be there to serve people. And volunteers just came along – most of them not even from the church. The wonderful thing was that serving in this way at this time changed the reputation of the church. It didn't just happen, it happened intentionally – we reached out and served because it's the work of Christ and we know that the work of Christ will always have a positive impact.

When the Covid-19 pandemic passed, Bishop Graham Tomlin named St Eth's as one of the Kensington area's fastest growing churches.

As you plan your plant, think about how you can make social justice part of your DNA, what initiatives you will put into place, and when you will start them.

MANAGING CHANGE

Church planting involves change, and as church planters it is helpful to consider managing that change. Despite this, we naturally find change quite difficult. Most of us prefer predictability, and we don't like the unexpected. When change is around, fear can increase, which in turn creates an inertia that can stop good things from happening. The ability to manage that change, wisely and strategically, is key to the church planter's role and can determine whether a plant succeeds or not. In any church plant, change happens in a number of ways. A team undergoes a move from a safe, structured place surrounded by friends to a place where everything is different, uncomfortable, and unfamiliar. How do we help the team, and those outside the team, make those changes?

This is particularly important when thinking about a graft; revitalising a church through a partnership. A graft seeks to help a smaller, insecure congregation (who may perceive change as loss) encounter an incoming group of people who are young and energetic. How can you help that older/established congregation receive this new influx, and help the incoming group manage a transition which involves coming up against people who might find this change challenging?

I believe this needs thinking through from a leadership point of view, primarily because leaders will be managing the changes that people experience. You may already be familiar with William Bridges' Old-Land-New-Land model for change that pictures a movement from 'the old land'

– the way things used to be – to 'the new land' – the place the change is heading towards. The image below can help people express where they are on the journey – which they might perceive as exciting and invigorating (sailing on a yacht, watching dolphins) or scary and dangerous (clinging to the raft, terrified of the sharks). As leaders, we need to be aware that people will experience different elements of change and allowing them to be heard and understood can dissipate much of the fear. This is particularly important if you are revitalising a church where there is an existing congregation.

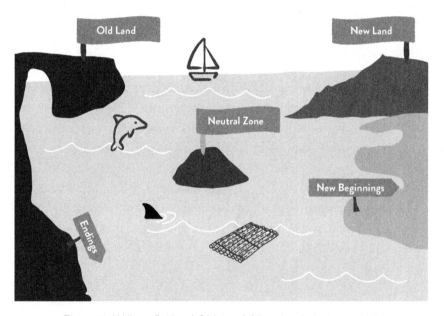

Figure 11: William Bridges' Old-Land-New-Land change model:
where are you in the change?

As part of your planning, anticipate different reactions to what is happening and patiently provide the space for others to articulate their thoughts and feelings.

COMMUNICATING WITH YOUR TEAM

At the heart of delivering well-made plans is good communication. It is essential at every level and at every point of what you are doing. How will you ensure you are communicating well with everyone involved? Consider weekly meetings with the sending church leader; weekly prayer and planning meetings with your core team; fortnightly vision and prayer meetings with the plant team; a weekly e-newsletter to team and supporters to keep them in the loop. Establish early on what kind of IT solution you will use so you can start using it even before the launch. If you're starting small, a social media group will be fine. As you grow, or if you are starting bigger, then you might need a bespoke package like ChurchSuite, Church App, or ChurchDesk to help organise the data well and communicate effectively.

START PLANNING!

Winston Churchill once said, 'Those who plan do better than those who do not plan, even should they rarely stick to their plan.' The point of planning is to be ready for what lies ahead, even if we cannot anticipate every eventuality. Planning gives you confidence to face complex tasks, and church planting can become complex! Circumstances are sometimes hard to control, but planning helps you prepare for the unexpected and all that might happen in practice. Surely the solution is to put in all the effort of planning, but to hold your plans loosely, submitting them to the Lord: 'Many are the plans in a person's heart, but it is the Lord's purpose that prevails.'[17]

17 Proverbs 19:21.

CALL TO ACTION: PLANNING

- Fill out the Leader's Map as much as you can and make note of the areas where your strategy needs more development.
- Develop your timeline.
- When could you start new ministries or activities in a staggered way rather than all at once?
- Who are your current stakeholders? What engagement do you need with them?
- In your experience, how have people come to faith? How will you be intentional about evangelism?
- What are the discipleship pathways you will develop to mature people in their faith?
- How will all this be simple and easily understood?
- If you are doing a revitalisation or a 'graft' ask yourself, how will you integrate the existing congregation and the new team?

4
CONTEXT

HOW TO ADAPT YOUR PLANT TO ITS CONTEXT

The great 19th-century missionary and founder of the China Inland Mission, Hudson Taylor, travelled to Shanghai to share the gospel. Initially, he was badly received as he preached and gave out medical supplies and offered his skills as a doctor. Taylor discovered that wherever he went he was being referred to as a 'black devil' because of the Western-style overcoat he was wearing. He decided to adopt Chinese clothes, shaved his forehead and wore a pigtail, following local customs, and consequently he had a better hearing. From then on, his mission work began to grow in impact and favour. Contextualisation is taking into account the context you are moving into and recognising that it may be very different to the one you came from.

An understanding of the principle of contextualisation or inculturation is an essential part of church planting in any place. It enables faithful Christian discipleship in a new cultural context rather than imposing a culture on that context from outside. This is one of the great learnings of the global missionary movement. And it is applicable as much at home as it is overseas. Bishop and missionary Lesslie Newbigin pointed out that the Church in the West has a special challenge because this is the first time it has had to mount a mission to a culture that was previously Christian.[1] Less than 8 per cent of people now go to church in the UK. Less than 1.6 per cent go to Anglican churches regularly.

So there is a great need to plant new churches to reach new people in new ways, right on our doorsteps. When we plant churches, we need to consider the place and the people we are going to. That will involve researching the context. It will also involve considering what kind or model of church plant is needed. And we will need to consider what kind

1 Lesslie Newbigin, *Foolishness to the Greeks: The Gospel and Western Culture* (Grand Rapids, MI: Eerdmans, 1986).

of physical space is going to best suit the missional needs of the people we are trying to reach.

PLACE

As church planters, we must wrestle with the theology of place. The incarnation of Jesus Christ points towards the discovery that he is found everywhere, in the here and now. Our encounters with place are framed through this lens. Certainly in England, any understanding of what is happening spiritually in a place today requires an understanding of the part the church has played in that place too – a kind of ecclesiastical geography.[2] Treating people without consideration of place misses huge insights into understanding them and how to connect them with the gospel.

Place can inform our vision. Gas Street Church, Birmingham, planted in 2016, found that their new church location became intimately bound up with their vision:

> When we first walked into the building that is now Gas Street Church we discovered that it was once an industrial site for the purpose of manufacturing gas that was used to power street lamps across the city. The history of the building instantly provided us with a compelling narrative, a prophetic picture, of a church that would be **light for the city.**

RESEARCH

As you prayer-walk and talk to local people, you can discover a lot about an area, but to get a more accurate understanding of the whole area, you need to do some systematic research. Research is important to help you understand more about the people around you, to highlight areas of need, to see how an area has changed over time and how it might change in the future, and, done properly, it can provide you with a starting point for measuring your impact on an area. If you are doing funding applications, research data helps build your case and helps measure what you are trying to do. Research is good for looking at the big picture, but sometimes God might want you to focus on something

2 Andrew Rumsey argues in his book, *Parish: An Anglican theology of place* (London: SCM, 2017), that any understanding of the Church of England, nationally and locally, requires ecclesiastical geography as much as ecclesiastical history.

that data does not say is important, so we need to exercise godly wisdom and prayerful insight as we do our research.

There are many ways to research an area and it is good to use several different approaches to see how they interrelate. Below are seven key areas to explore, with some pointers to some of the excellent data sources that are available online:

1. **Physical** – Get to know the geography of your area. Make a map and identify the institutions, shops, restaurants, local businesses, housing areas. What are the physical barriers like major roads or train tracks? What are the thoroughfares and places where people hang out? Explore the statistical geography to get proportions of the above.

2. **Social** – Who are the people in your area? Who are the people God is calling you to focus on? It might be the whole parish if you are doing a parish revitalisation, or it might be a specific group in the community who you have identified as an 'unreached' group who need to encounter God's love. Some places to start looking at this are the Office for National Statistics (ONS), including their 10-yearly census data, the Church of England's mapping tool, and the Church Urban Fund 'online lookup' tool.

3. **Organisational** – How is your area organised? Who else has influence in your community? Who else is at work here? What do they do? Some data on this can be found on Nomis, a service provided by ONS, and also on local council websites, but also search local forums and business and community networks online and in social media.[3]

4. **Strategic** – What might happen in the future in your community? Search online for your local borough council or county council's Local Plan. In Tower Hamlets, we had access to a 25-year planning document which was extremely helpful to know about. More locally, get to know or join your own neighbourhood planning forums. Other groups might have their own local strategies too.

3 See these resources: https://www.ons.gov.uk/census; https://www.nomisweb.co.uk/reports/localarea; https://www.churchofengland.org/about/data-services; and https://cuf.org.uk/lookup-tool.

5. **Historical** – What is the story of your community? The East End of London, for instance, has been marked by immigration and people movement since the Huguenots' arrival in the 1790s, followed by European Jewish communities in the 20th century and more recently by Bangladeshi Muslims. The Second World War blitz had a massive impact on housing. The development of deep sea container ships requiring deeper docks led to many East Enders moving out to Essex for work. The development of Canary Wharf as a new financial business district in London has changed the demographics further still. These all have an impact on local experience and the feel of a place.

6. **Relational** – What are relationships in your community like? How is your church and other churches seen by your community? How are you perceived by other churches and other organisations? You could use surveys or simply ask direct questions.

7. **Spiritual** – What is God doing in your area? Who are the other church leaders in your area – in your own denomination and others – and what is their story? One of the most common comments I hear from church planters is that they thought they were 'bringing God to a neighbourhood' only to discover that he was already there, waiting to be discovered. So what has God been doing in your community? Whose shoulders are you standing on? How does God see your community? What is the vision that God has given you for the area?

Commission members of your team to research the area for the plant and create a profile document. Share this more widely and prayerfully take time to draw out some of the insights that it provides. Then use this to enhance and develop your vision and strategy.

MAPPING – WHO ARE WE NOT REACHING?

An important research question to ask early on is a missional one: who are we not reaching? As Anglicans, we have a vision to have a church for every neighbourhood in the country. This is at the heart of the parish system, where every soul is part of a parish. However, when we look at our churches and our parishes or neighbourhoods, we quickly realise that there are swathes of people we are not touching with the gospel. This is especially true of urban areas that have dense populations.

I have done extensive work with deaneries (groupings of parishes) to help them develop church planting strategies for their areas. They draw a map of their area, and (only for the sake of this exercise) remove parish boundaries, then clergy and local leaders identify smaller areas or people groups who they do not have connections with. They might discover particular age profiles which are unrepresented in the church. The missional question then is how do we reach them with the good news of Jesus. That will involve some kind of intentional strategy which might lead to an invitation or a decision to do something new to reach the people in that new place. This kind of mapping exercise is highly energising missionally and naturally leads to intercession and reflection on what to do. I encourage deaneries to create a long list of possibilities and then to pray over a short list and then to make a plan to implement. It could be as simple as starting a new congregation in an existing church to reach a new group of people, or starting something in a new place, reaching new people in new ways.

A research and mapping process was used to great effect by a team from St George-in-the-East, a resource church in the Catholic tradition, partnering with the Centre for Theology and Community (CTC) to start a church for workers in the City of London. This process began with prayer-walking around a part of the parish which bordered the City of London, asking people working and living there what the church could be for them. They found themselves talking to many low-paid workers in the hospitality and construction sectors, and it soon became clear that there was an opportunity to deepen this engagement. A small team of lay 'Mission Chaplains' was put together to extend the listening process over more than a year and the whole parish was invited to join in, including a prayer-walk by the children to see what they noticed. This patient process revealed, among other things, a particular need for English classes at the weekend, worship on Saturdays in other languages, and a desire to gather with other workers to actively build a sense of community. This all would require a space in the City, and God provided the historic Guild Church for Workers on Leadenhall Street, St Katharine Cree, that I mentioned in chapter 3.

What began as an exploration through simply listening became a renewal of a City church refocused on particular demographics of low-paid, often migrant, workers, shaping the worship and outreach around their needs. There are now services in Spanish, carol services for cleaners, and growing involvement in taking action to help more workers earn a real living wage – and the free Saturday English classes continue to grow. This research and mapping process helped them to discern who God was trying to reach in that place, and how to do so.

Fiona Mayne had a different experience of research and mapping. She lives in Haywood Village in Weston-super-Mare, a new housing estate with no church. After becoming a Christian, she began to ask people in her community what they wanted for the estate, and they said that they 'wanted somewhere to meet up.' So, with other local Christians, she began 'Take Five,' a pop-up café in a school community room. An Alpha group organically emerged from the 100-strong attendees of the café. People began to ask where the church in Haywood Village was, so she asked them what they wanted it to look like. They said, 'like Take Five but with Christian content.' Hearing this, Fiona began Tea & Toast Church in the hall, a café-style church service. They continue to run Alpha and now also have a weekly evening of discussion and prayer over a meal. All of this emerged from Fiona asking people in her community the right questions and responding to their answers.[4]

This leads us to ask what is the right kind of church for the place we are going to? What 'model' or approach is most appropriate?

ATTRACTIONAL OR MISSIONAL?

This approach raises a question of how contextual a church plant should be. This is an ongoing debate in mission circles that explores whether a church is attractional or missional at its heart.

An attractional approach to church focuses its primary purpose on attracting unchurched and disengaged Christians to come to Jesus and connect or reconnect with the Church. It is invitational at its heart. These churches develop strong services and focus on their outward-facing ministries, putting time and resources into creating vibrant worship

---

4 A story from *Send Me: Stories of ordinary people planting new churches*, edited by John McGinley (London: CCX, 2023).

experiences, dynamic programmes, and engaging events. For example, in the Anglo-Catholic tradition, St Laurence's Church, Chorley holds an all-age Mass with contemporary music at 5 p.m. on Saturdays, because Sunday mornings are not necessarily a good time for everyone. They have managed to establish a brand new congregation at this service, with numbers regularly reaching 100 people of all ages.

On the other hand, a missional approach to church emphasises going to where people are rather than expecting them to come to church. This approach recognises the cultural barriers that some experience of walking into a church building or encountering an overtly Christian context. It focuses on going out beyond the church walls and actively engaging in the world beyond. This more contextual approach means that missional models of church might look very different to gathered ones.

In my view, there is no one 'correct' approach – we need both! Both seek to bring the love of Jesus to their communities, meet their needs, and share the gospel through acts of service and relationship building, but they do it in different ways. The only question to consider is, what will best fit the context you are seeking to plant in? The church model must be adapted to its context, and this will affect your planting strategy.

MODELS OF CHURCH PLANT

One of the challenges when exploring what kind of model is required is that there is such a wide range of possibilities and approaches to planting. The language involved is sometimes contested as different planters and pioneers focus passionately on their own particular emphases. I categorise planters into three broad categories: 'church plants,' 'fresh expressions of church,' and 'disciple-making movements.' This is not the place for an extended treatise on these, but I include a brief overview to help us orientate and navigate this space:

- **Church plants** have the aim of starting a worshipping community from the beginning, using a style and approach that is brought with them from their sending church.

- **Fresh expressions of church** have the aim of reaching a new community by serving them first, making disciples, and forming church as it emerges, rather than bringing any particular model of church from elsewhere.

● **Disciple-making movements** have the aim of making disciples who make disciples in a multiplying way and churches are formed as these disciples gather together and multiply in a similar way.

My perspective is that each of these movements have very different approaches to mission and that they can all work in the same mission field. They are all passionate about that mission and passionate about their approaches. They are also reaching different people in the different models they use. So we need them all! In practice, some churches adopt all of these approaches at various points while others focus on just one.

Why is all this important to include here? In the planting I have done personally, we recognised the need to diversify our approach locally as well as regionally because some approaches are more appropriate than others in particular contexts, but overall the mission is so great that we need every kind of approach to reach everyone. This multifaceted approach reflects the creativity of God, the broad body of Christ, and the many tribes of the kingdom of God. While there is likely to be one approach that seems best to you, it is also good to know about others so you can explore them if necessary, affirm them if working alongside them, and bless them as we all seek God's kingdom on earth.

Different approaches to planting and pioneering lead to different kinds of new worshipping communities being created. Pioneer thinkers Tina Hodgett and Paul Bradbury have categorised different kinds of planting according to the impulse of the lead planter. They recognised the very different mindsets involved from different kinds of pioneer and brought common language to this part of the Church's mission. When a model of church plant is chosen, it contextualises according to the approach that that leader adopts. Hodgett and Bradbury describe four different kinds of planters:[5]

1. **Church replicators** who bring what has worked elsewhere and start it afresh in a new place. This includes parish church revitalisations and plants that look and feel like the church

5 https://churchmissionsociety.org/anvil/pioneering-mission-is-a-spectrum-tina-hodgett-and-paul-bradbury-anvil-vol-34-issue-1/.

they were sent from. Pioneers now call this group **Pioneer reproducers** because no two churches are ever the same.

2. **Pioneer adaptors** who adapt an existing model of church in a new context. This might include Messy Churches that host unchurched families using a hands-on approach to worship, and café churches that have elements of worship, teaching, and fellowship.

3. **Pioneer innovators** who start with serving a community, building relationships, offering disciple-making, and then allowing the response to shape the church community that emerges. This includes missional communities, neo-monastic communities, and emergent churches. Innovators follow a process similar to the Fresh Expressions journey I discuss elsewhere in this book.

4. **Pioneer activists** who start social enterprises and businesses using Christian principles and motives with a view to influence the world in a positive way for God's glory. This includes so-called 'kingdom businesses' that might enable or host other Christian activity.

It is important to reassert that churches are communities of followers of Jesus, not buildings or worship services, although those do form part of the visible expression of the local Christian community when it gathers. The former is the living, breathing, dynamic essence of that group of Christians; it is the body of Christ in that locality; it is the people of God in that place. Choosing the right model recognises all of these dynamics and it will shape that community profoundly.

So with all the above in mind, here are some of the models of church that are commonly being used in the UK, with some examples you can follow up on to see what they look like in practice:

1. **New developments** – A new church community established within a new residential development that has a distinct sense of community or that is not easily served by an existing church. For example, Concord Church, Bristol was planted to reach the new development at Filton Airfield, which was where the Concorde aircraft was designed and built. It draws on the history of pioneering to reach its new community.

2. **Reopening closed churches** – A leader and congregation are invited to 'plant' into a church building that is either closed, facing closure, or needs so much help to survive that a different approach is needed and agreed. For example, St Werburgh's, Derby was closed for a number of decades, with the space being used most recently as a large Chinese restaurant. It was bought back, redeveloped for ministry, and planted into to re-establish a Christian community in that place. It has gone on to revitalise St Francis on the Mackworth Estate and St Edmund's Allenton and Shelton Lock with planting teams.

3. **Parish revitalisation** – A leader and a congregation 'graft' into an existing congregation with a view to infusing the church with new DNA and fresh energy. This is a partnership between old and new, but with the understanding of change being welcomed. For example, the Bishop of Edmonton invited Christchurch Mayfair to send a leader and a planting team to 'graft' into the small but willing congregation at St Paul's Haringey. This has given them the energy and momentum to grow and flourish with new life. St George's Preston is a great example in the traditional Anglo-Catholic tradition. The church was revitalised in partnership with the neighbouring Preston Minster (which itself was revitalised by HTB), specifically to reach out to those with no current church connection, including local students.

4. **New congregation** – Developing a new service for a new people group within the existing parish church. This will include international congregations, perhaps using their own languages. For example, St Matthew's Elephant and Castle started a Spanish-speaking Sunday Mass alongside their English-language congregation to gather and reach out to the many Spanish-speaking people in the community. They describe themselves as a 'bi-lingual community of faith.'

5. **Network church** – A leader and a congregation start a new church in a new space that draws in people through their network of relationships. This is not a geographic (parish) church but exists autonomously within or across another parish or number of

parishes. For example, Exeter Network Church was planted to reach young people in Exeter. They have a Bishop's Mission Order with a mandate to reach the whole city. They hired their own building and have grown significantly and gone on to plant a variety of churches in different contexts: Love the Street Church, meeting in homes; an afternoon congregation called StMatts@5 in a nearby parish; a rural church called St Basil's meeting on a farm; and a parish revitalisation at St Boniface, Whipton, a local suburb.

6.   **School plant** – A new worshipping community based within and ministering to a school community in its broadest sense and not just using a school building as a venue for worship. For example, Grace Church Highlands, planted from Christchurch Cockfosters with a team of 30 adults and children into Highlands School. At the time of writing, the Church of England's Flourish initiative is beginning to plant new Christian communities in schools across the country.

7.   **Estate church** – A church based on an un(der)reached estate that has a distinct sense of community and a distinct ministry to that estate. For example, Helen Shannon gathered a team who asked, 'What would the Strawberry Vale Estate look like if the kingdom of God invaded it?!' They started church@five and now train other estate church planters to go to the many unreached estates in London.

8.   **Café church** – Creating new congregations in 'third spaces', especially in cafés and coffee shops. In some places, running the coffee shop may also pay for the mission work. Third spaces are understood as being a space distinct from 'first spaces' (homes) and 'second spaces' (workplaces), such as cafés, restaurants, etc. For example, St Giles Codicote, a rural church in Hertfordshire, has a monthly café church. They open up the village hall and invite the community to come for breakfast and a short service, with songs, crafts, and a short reflection. Lots of families come, including many who don't usually go to church.

9.   **Workplace church** – A worshipping community based in a workplace ('second space') connecting with those who work

there. St Helen's Bishopsgate has planted many lunchtime services in the City of London with the intention of creating an outward-looking church community within a five-minute walk of their workplace. I was involved in a chaplaincy at Harrods for a few years, ministering to the 5,000-strong workforce based in that store. They met on Wednesday lunchtimes for worship and fellowship and hosted evangelistic carol services at Christmas, along with wonderful Harrods mince pies donated by the store!

10. **Missional/Pioneer communities** – These are understood as communities constituted by a specific missional purpose in relation to a network or a place. They are not parish churches or places of conventional worship. Many of these are now developing into small church communities with their own identity. They often meet in homes and are sometimes referred to as 'micro-churches.' For example, St Peter's Bourne is a missional community in North London. They are a diverse group of Christians who intentionally live together to follow this rule of life: 'Pursuing God and learning to serve in mission together.' They have three focuses: they are a centre of prayer for North London; a catalyst for developing meaningful social action among marginalised people; and a catalyst and training hub for pioneer missioners in North London.

11. **Messy Church or similar** – This is a way of being church for families, not just children. It is adaptable to its context but its values are about being Christ-centred, for all ages, based on creativity, hospitality, and celebration. For example, Lucy Moore started the first Messy Church at St Wilfrid's Cowplain because they weren't connecting with local families. Since then, thousands of Messy Churches have been 'planted' – across the country and abroad.

12. **Age-related churches** – These focus on creating churches for a particular age group such as children, youth, young adults, or senior citizens. For example, Unlimited Church, Exeter[6]

6 Their story has been written in founding leader Liz Grier's book, *Beginning Unlimited: The Diary of a Church Plant* (Rickmansworth: Instant Apostle, 2018).

was planted in 2010 as part of an initiative to connect with the many young people in Exeter who have little or no experience of church and more importantly of faith and Jesus. In the Catholic tradition, Lighthouse Service at St Peter and St Paul Rishton is a 3 p.m. Sunday afternoon family-focused Mass which has grown to about 60 regulars.

13. **Special interest groups** – These tend to be new congregations which initially aim to connect incarnationally with a particular group, such as those who might play a particular sport or have a certain hobby. For example, Choir Church involves a church running an after-school choir, led by a director of music. It teaches music to a high level, but is grounded in prayer and worship, with a vision to build a congregation. Clergy, lay workers, parents, and volunteers are also involved each week. At a choir session, children learn anthems and hymns, and more broadly about worship, faith, and sacraments. Once a month, this prayerful preparation culminates in a midweek Eucharist in the school hall, making them active participants in musical worship, joined by parents and friends. Choir Church was first planted in the parish of St George-in-the-East and there are now many around the country, for example in the Anglo-Catholic parish of Holy Trinity Tarleton.

14. **New monastic communities** – These communities include a stronger focus on intentional community through a gathered and dispersed life, patterns of prayer, contemplation, hospitality, and practical engagement in mission beyond itself (often to the poor). For example, St Thomas' Community, a fresh expression of church with a rhythm of life based around prayer, mission, and hospitality, ministering to an inner-city area of around 25,000 people in Derby. Their community is focused on working in urban areas, intensifying people's discipleship, serving the mission of the local church, and growing the kingdom of God.

15. **Resource churches** – These are churches that are designated by their bishop as church-planting churches in city centres, city regions, or town centres. They work strategically with the bishop with an

expectation that they will plant churches in other parts of the city and further afield to other cities and towns. Resource churches may be created by planting a new church or by designating an existing large church as a resource church.[7] For example, Harbour Church, Portsmouth, appointed by the Bishop of Portsmouth to revitalise churches in the diocese and planted from St Peter's Brighton initially into a department store. They have revitalised parish churches in Portsmouth, Gosport, and the Isle of Wight. Other encouraging examples include St Philip's Salford, St Thomas' Newcastle, and St Thomas' Norwich.

The Myriad programme that has emerged from the Gregory Centre trains lay people to plant a new worshipping community using a number of the models above. Many Myriad communities have been planted around the country with the aim of training and planting thousands more. These lay planters are overseen by their parish priest, or equivalent, who provides guidance, governance, accountability, and support for these embryonic new communities. These plants then find their place within the wider church, for example, through the diocese commissioning them.[8]

MEETING SPACES

Where you meet has a massive impact on the people you will reach. Iconic church buildings will attract some people and put off others. Meeting in a school or a café works favourably for some but doesn't feel like church for others. What will enable rather than inhibit the kind of worshipping community you are aiming to plant? Will your gatherings be formal or informal, your worship buoyant praise or more quiet contemplation? Do you need a small space to start, like someone's home, or something bigger from the outset? There are almost always compromises to be made and you may need to moderate your expectations. Here are some things to consider when you are looking to plant to a particular place or community:

- **Visibility** – Is the church location visible? One parish church in London is tucked away down a drive off a minor road, rendering it

7 For more, see Ric Thorpe, *Resource Churches* (London: CCX, 2021).
8 For more details, visit www.ccx.org.uk/myriad-lay-led-planting/.

completely invisible unless you know where to find the sign to show you the way. Or is your building on a high street for all to see?

- **Accessibility** – Is it accessible for those with disabilities? Is it close to a road? Does it have enough parking? Are there public transport links nearby?

- **Size** – Is it big enough for the vision of what God is calling you to do? Or is it too big?

- **Main meeting room** – Are there pews or other fixed furniture limiting what is possible during the week?

- **Rooms** – Are there enough small group rooms for children's groups, courses like Alpha, or prayer meetings?

- **Offices** – Is there office space with internet access?

- **Storage** – Is there enough space for chairs, tables, children's church resources, signage, PA systems, etc?

- **Power supplies** – Is there enough power to run lights, sound, and hot drinks facilities?

- **Kitchen** – Is there a place to do catering for courses or refreshments for gathered worship?

- **State of repair** – Does the building need expensive one-off repairs or large maintenance costs?

- **Running costs** – Do you have an idea how much the room or buildings cost to run per year, including heating, lighting, and cleaning?

- **Beauty** – Is it an attractive building or an ugly one? For some this is important. How easy will it be to make changes to it?

These requirements are rarely all met and you will need to balance pros against cons. Don't feel bound to one option. The Diocese of Birmingham agreed with Gas Street Church to buy a warehouse inside the parish where there was already a church building. The building was fully paid off within a few years and fulfils the needs of this large city centre resource church. They continue to use the parish church building too.

Sharon Collins, a lay planter in Blackburn, originally planted an estate church in a community library. During the Covid-19 pandemic they moved onto an abandoned allotment at the centre of the estate, meeting under a polytunnel. They continue to use both the community library and the allotment for worship and church activities. The space of the allotment is especially core to their mission. Sharon says:

> I think there's something so important about doing things in public spaces; people are always walking right past for a start. One guy came in with his daughter because he heard us all laughing! He wouldn't have come in if he'd had to push a door open. I'm not saying that all churches should be outside but it works for us.[9]

New Life Church, Breightmet, part of the Antioch Network in Manchester Diocese, meets in the function room of a pub on an estate in Bolton. It is a church plant within the existing parish of Christ Church Harwood. Wendy Oliver, the now-retired vicar of Christ Church, said that the parish church was struggling to reach people on the estate. Some people on the estate saw it as the 'pretty church on top of the hill' which had no interest in them. For 14 years Wendy and others prayed for a plant in the estate, until Ben and Amy Woodfield felt called and then planted a worshipping community into a local pub. That pub is at the heart of the estate, and highly accessible to the people there. They feel it's a church for them.

The space you choose, or find yourself in, becomes part of your story. It shapes your community and your mission. Whether it is an old parish church, a warehouse, or a polytunnel, God promises to be with us because we are gathering in his name.[10]

SETTLING IN

Your context is everything. You might have sacrificed a great deal and perhaps left friends and family to pour yourself into a new place. When my family moved to Shadwell in East London, it was new in almost every way – culturally, demographically, geographically. We left a strong church community, school friends, and familiar places and there was a sense of loss which we all felt for some time. God had called us to go but it took

9 A story from *Send Me: Stories of ordinary people planting new churches*, edited by John McGinley (London: CCX, 2023).
10 Matthew 18:20.

three years for us to start calling Shadwell 'home.' What changed? We began to make friends, understand that new community, and came to love the people there deeply. Settling into a new context means to take the time to understand it, to grow to love the people there and see them through God's eyes. It's then that we discover that God was there all along and we are simply joining in with him.

CALL TO ACTION: CONTEXT

Using the internet and other resources, create a profile of the place you're planting into:

- **Physical:** geography
- **Social:** statistics
- **Organisational:** who, what, and how
- **Strategic:** planning documents
- **Historical:** what is the story of your community?
- **Relational:** what are your relationships like?
- **Spiritual:** what is God doing?

Explore how you will listen to your community and to God in your plant, by considering your answers to the following questions:

- Which different groups of people live or work in the parish or area around the plant?
- What expressions of church might you develop to reach them?
- How might these expressions of church help you develop your main act of worship?

5
AUTHORITY

HOW TO PLANT WITH PERMISSION AND SUPPORT

This chapter is always going to be complicated, as we all have different experiences of authority, positive or negative. Whether we like it or not, power is at work and we need to pay attention to it carefully.

We know that God is the ultimate authority and that any power we have is given by him, but that power can be used well or abused badly. It can be used to build up or tear down. It can create freedom or it can control and manipulate. Many of us today distrust those in authority over us. While politicians, advertising executives, government ministers, estate agents, and journalists are the five least-trusted professions, clergy and church leaders are still only trusted by 55 per cent of the population.[1] Sadly, some have experienced abusive leadership in their churches too.

So the question for this chapter is, how do we make sure we are working well with authority? How do we ensure that power dynamics are recognised and used appropriately? How do we lead in such a way that people are safer and healthier? How do we make sure that the governance structures and lines of authority are in place to protect us and those we lead? Safeguarding in plants is covered in chapter 8 on Resources.

The New Testament has a lot to say about learning to use authority and leading well, whatever position you find yourself in. Two verses stand out for me in this:

> *Have confidence in your leaders and submit to their authority, because they keep watch over you as those who must give an account. Do this so that their work will be a joy, not a burden, for that would be of no benefit to you. (Hebrews 13:17)*

---

1 Ipsos Veracity Index 2022, https://www.ipsos.com/en-uk/ipsos-veracity-index-2022.

In the same way, you who are younger, submit yourselves to your elders. All of you, clothe yourselves with humility towards one another, because, 'God opposes the proud but shows favour to the humble.' (1 Peter 5:5)

The writer to the Hebrews and St Peter both encourage the good use of authority by leaders and submission to that authority by those who follow. When it works well, joy and benefits abound. And St Paul encourages everyone to have an attitude of humility in this: 'Submit to one another out of reverence for Christ.'[2]

I have seen enthusiastic church planters step outside their authority which can then create tension with the sending church leadership. For example, if the church planter invites the highest giver and key members of staff to join them on the plant team without talking this through with the senior leader, this will create mistrust and tension. Or, if a sending church announces a church revitalisation without fully working it through with the local bishop how that might be received in the place they are going to, there is a strong likelihood of unnecessary miscommunication and pastoral issues. In both cases, the church planter has stepped outside the authority they have and would be avoided by talking it through with those who carry that authority.

Let's look at these important lines of authority and how they can work out in practice.

BISHOPS AND NETWORK LEADERS

Most denominations and church networks have some kind of hierarchical oversight structure. In the Church of England, dioceses are overseen by bishops who have spiritual and temporal authority over the churches in that area. As the diocesan bishop is chief pastor of the diocese, spiritual authority is given by them to parish clergy to lead services, occasional offices (weddings, funerals, etc), preaching, teaching, and holding the cure of souls (pastoral care). The temporal aspects of their authority gives legal possession of the parish property, with the right to manage the property and control the parish. If a church plant is happening within the parish, for example, planting in order to reach another part of the parish

2 Ephesians 5:21.

geographically, then the responsibility and authority for the plant lies with the parish priest. If it is outside the parish, and by definition in someone else's parish, the bishop must give authority for the plant, whether it is a parish revitalisation or another plant, requiring a Bishop's Mission Order (see models of church plant in the previous chapter).

In other denominations or networks, you need to explore where the lines of authority lie so that you can make sure you are not stepping outside your own authority. Even in independent church networks spread across the country, there will be protocols which are there not to stop this activity but to ensure it is done well and with reference to others.

In my experience, it is good to talk to the bishop, or oversight leader, as early as possible in the process. There may well be information that a bishop might hold that would be very helpful to know about early in the decision-making process, as well as the bishop appreciating your own desire to plant. I had an early meeting with Bishop Stephen Oliver, Area Bishop of Stepney, when we first planted into the area, where he asked me whether we would like to help other churches through planting and revitalising. He opened up a map of East London and showed me five or six places that he wanted to see supported over time. Within eight years of that conversation, God had opened the door to four of them for us to plant into. We were delighted to plant and give away leaders, people, and money for the sake of the Church in East London, but it would not have been possible without the bishop enabling it.

Archie Coates, now vicar of HTB, reflects on how he did this while planting St Peter's in Brighton. He saw himself as a partner in the gospel with the Bishop and Diocese of Chichester. He says:

> Each time I met him, I would ask my bishop if I could help with anything. All bishops are spinning multiple plates and they all want to see their churches grow. In our diocese, church buildings were being closed, which the locals didn't want but no priests were applying. So we partnered with the diocese and were able to be part of the solution.

Partnering with your bishop is more than proper procedure, it can lead to amazing opportunities for church multiplication. In the Church of England, talking to the appropriate people at the right time is important for making things happen in the right way and keeping people informed in helpful ways rather than discovering through an alternative route. So talk to your bishop about the best way to approach each group of stakeholders (you can use the stakeholder chart from chapter 3 on Planning). This will usually include archdeacons, area deans, immediate clergy neighbours, deanery chapters, and synods – lots of people, but if you get it right, they will be able to support you rather than hinder you.

SENDING CHURCH LEADER

Perhaps the most critical relationship to get right is between the church planter and the sending church leader. Ideally, this should be one of openness, generosity, and mutual respect. However, I have seen some cases where hiddenness, frugality, and suspicion dominate these relationships and they inevitably lead to troubled waters ahead.

If you are the sending church leader, this is a wonderful opportunity to see kingdom multiplication as a result of your obedience, courage, and generosity. Seize the moment to do it well. I would encourage you to take the initiative in the whole process with regular meetings with the church planter, acting more as a coach than as a boss. Your role is to help them get ready and enable them to do the best possible job that they can do. Work out an agenda for your meetings across the months ahead leading up to the plant, perhaps using this book as a guide for the questions you need to explore. Set a positive, encouraging, respectful tone to the meetings and agree that they should be goal-orientated with a measure of accountability. It is important early on to clarify expectations:

1. Consider what time the planter will need each week to research and prepare well for the plant.

2. Consider what responsibilities should continue meanwhile in the sending church, and how to finish well.

3. Discuss the size of the team the planter is hoping to take – see chapter 6 – it is important not to send too many from the sending church. Sandy Millar advised not to 'kill the goose that lays the golden egg' – if too many leave it can set the sending church back years in terms of recovering from a plant. It is equally important not to send too few – the plant needs momentum to get it going so it needs a realistic size for success.

4. Discuss the names of particular people the planter would like to invite – before inviting them! It is courteous and wise to do this. There could be unknown issues, or it might be a matter of bad timing as it could impact others.

5. Agree to discuss with the sending church leader any person who asks the planter direct if they can join the team.

6. Discuss and decide whether the plant and sending church will ever gather together for large occasions. Will there be any joint prayer meetings?

7. Use this space to honestly address hopes and fears in a safe place.

8. Encourage deep foundations of prayer – it is too easy to take matters into your own hands, which leads to trouble, rather than trusting God.

9. Be honest about any disappointments or if things don't go as expected to avoid any later misunderstandings.

10. Clarify expectations around how long you will continue to meet in this way.

When communication is clear and expectations are clarified, this relationship with a sending church can be supportive, encouraging, and releasing.

GOVERNANCE AND LEADERSHIP STRUCTURES

The Church of England considers good governance to be 'an enabler of effectiveness, a shaper of culture, an assurance to stakeholders that the resources entrusted to the organisation have been used appropriately and should reflect what the Church calls virtue in its focus on truth and integrity'.[3] It makes sure that the church is safe and ordered, and that the people involved in leadership correctly implement that governance and reflect that overall aim.

The church planter needs to consider what leadership structures the new plant will need, whether it is a plant from scratch, or, for example,

3 Church of England Governance Review Update, GS Misc 1319, page 6, paragraph 5.

with a revitalisation plant, the need to develop and improve the current structures. This will vary according to your denomination.

If a Church of England parish church is planting a new Christian community in another part of the parish, then there needs to be clear lines of accountability from the planter (lay or ordained) to the parish priest and the PCC. If the plant is a revitalisation of another parish or an autonomous plant in another parish then it will need specific governance and leadership structures. I will address this later.

I have found it helpful to think about the three groups that hold leadership roles in a parish church. Firstly, there is the PCC (the trustees of the church charity) which has overall responsibility for governance and vision. They work with the church leader to ensure good governance, financial accountability, buildings upkeep, staff employment, and safeguarding. Secondly, there are the pastoral leaders, who might be ordained or not, leading small groups and ministries in the church. Finally, there might be a staff team which looks after the day-to-day aspects of running the church. The church leader is of course in every group and there are some who are in more than one group. The important thing here is for each group to know its responsibilities and boundaries, in order to avoid confusion. The PCC can get bogged down in day-to-day matters – like the paint colour in the loos! – rather than focusing their attention on important governance decisions that can only be taken by them. The visual on the next page illustrates this:

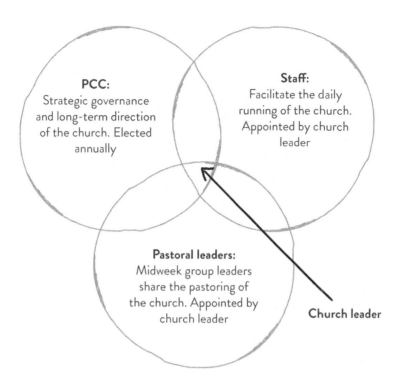

PCC:
Strategic governance
and long-term direction
of the church. Elected
annually

Staff:
Facilitate the daily
running of the church.
Appointed by church
leader

Pastoral leaders:
Midweek group leaders
share the pastoring of
the church. Appointed by
church leader

Church leader

Figure 12: Clarify where church governance, operational and pastoral leadership intersect

The main point of this is the division of focus and labour, with appropriate accountability keeping you on track with your vision and purpose, both internally within the church and externally within any wider accountability structure. Whether you use this particular structure or not, you will still need to consider how a plant fits within your governance and leadership structures, so that there is good communication and clear lines of authority.

LEGALITIES

There are two main legal structures in the Church of England that are used for planting: using existing parish structures when a parish church is revitalised; and a Bishop's Mission Order when there is a new initiative in someone else's parish. There are a few other options which I'll mention later, but these are the two most commonly used.

It is vital to make sure a plant is on a clear legal footing from the outset, including adherence to charity law. Ask an expert in your denomination

– an archdeacon in the Church of England – or get in touch with an organisation that specialises in supporting the charitable side of churches.[4]

In the Church of England, canon law enables the church to be governed well and helps clarify the most appropriate structures that will enable the church plant to thrive and work well with other local churches.

PLANTING TO REVITALISE A PARISH

For revitalising a parish church with a planting team, the legalities are exactly the same as for existing parish structures. You need permission from the bishop to plant into another parish. If you are becoming the parish priest of that new parish, with a church revitalisation team, then you will be appointed priest-in-charge and given a licence. The bishop will publicly appoint the church leader to take responsibility for that parish using the usual means of installation, induction, and licensing.

One challenge is that members of the incoming plant team are not able to stand for election onto the PCC until they have been members of the parish church for six months, in order to get onto the electoral roll in order to be voted onto the PCC. That means that crucial decisions about new services, budgets and spending, and any reordering of buildings can only be made by the existing PCC, acting as trustees. This does not make change easy for the first year or so and an interim arrangement will need to be made. You can co-opt up to one-third of a PCC from outside the electoral roll with full voting rights. A treasurer might be helpful to be in this group. Planning ahead, you might be able to have some people attend the church for at least six months before the plant so they can be elected onto the PCC in their own right. Wardens can be voted in immediately once they are on the electoral roll, and this will all need careful thought and planning.

PLANTING USING A BISHOP'S MISSION ORDER

If you are planting a church autonomously within another parish, the local bishop will need to create a Bishop's Mission Order (BMO). A legal instrument ('the mission order') is granted, by which the bishop endorses

4 Stewardship.co.uk, for example, helps churches to become charities under UK law.

and authorises the church plant to promote and further the mission of the Church in that place. There will be written and agreed 'protocols' which are talked through with the various stakeholders, including arrangements for worship, finances, and leadership. This may involve the creation of a charitable incorporated organisation (CIO) to enable the church to have a bank account – see chapter 8 on Resources for more on this.

The Order is best written by the archdeacon and is kept as simple and clear as possible. It may be accompanied by a supplementary instrument which adds details of a secondary nature, including governance arrangements, specific collaboration with other churches, links with a charity set up to support the plant which might also enable separate bank accounts to be used, etc. BMOs are usually reviewed within five years of being created and then made permanent, if not before.

It goes without saying that a BMO requires enormous sensitivity, humility, and collegiality on the part of the planter. Clarity is vital, especially if there are any leadership changes in the diocese over the first few years of the plant. Even though a BMO can have the legal authority to minister across many parishes, conflict with the local clergy could prevent the plant from thriving. Remember that even though you may have different understandings of church and theology, your local clergy love God and want to see his kingdom come in the world. They may feel threatened or worried at first, but do not let that get in the way of your partnership in the gospel. Work hard to support each other in your common goal so that you can be a blessing to your deanery and diocese.

Examples of BMOs in my own diocese include KXC, which is a network church drawing people across the Kings Cross area and beyond; church@ five, a church plant on a housing estate in Strawberry Vale, East Finchley, in collaboration with the parish church; St Luke's Millwall, a church plant into a daughter church of a large parish on the Isle of Dogs in London.

OTHER OPTIONS

Alternative legal structures have been used in the past and I cover them here in case you hear them mentioned as possible solutions. The first is to create an **extra-parochial place,** most likely to be useful where the new church is to be based permanently in a specific church building which needs to be able to operate without any need to refer to the local incumbent or any other church buildings.

At one time, **conventional districts** were regularly used for planting new churches. A conventional district is a designated area of one or more parishes which has its own minister and may have its own chapel/place of worship. They can be set up without much legal formality – all that is needed is a written agreement between the various people involved. In the past that made them attractive in cases where planting a new church was being tried out in a particular place for a few years before a decision was taken whether to put it on a permanent legal footing. As far as possible, keep things simple!

Churches that don't pay enough attention to governance get into trouble. Churches that grow very fast need to keep a close eye on governance and leadership structures to see how they need to adapt. What is right at the beginning almost certainly will need to change. I have seen examples of church plants growing exponentially without the structures in place to support that growth, and interventions have had to be made that could have been avoided if due diligence was in place. Most of these issues arise from naivety rather than anything underhand, but they are avoidable with regular consideration by the trustees.

COMING TO MATURITY

How long should a church plant be called a church plant? At what point is a church plant considered as a 'normal,' more mature church? Church plants are vulnerable in the early years because the deeper foundations that time and experience bring are still being established. But it is unhelpful to keep a church plant in this vulnerable state for too long by denying it the chance to become fully established and equal in status to other churches. Conversely, the church plant itself might feel that keeping its identity as a church plant is important for its own story and to stay missionally agile enough to keep being adaptable in its own context.

A church plant should be accountable to its own leaders, to its sending church, who have invested and given so much, and to its network or denomination. Again, it is helpful to discuss in advance the expectations of accountability:

- **For a bishop/overseer** – It is helpful to have someone appointed to the charity board of a BMO who represents, or stays connected, with the diocese/network. Parish revitalisations are already accountable as parish churches. Church planters should keep in touch with their bishop to give updates and share good news stories of what God is doing.

- **For a sending church leader** – Keep meeting the church planter as a coach or mentor for the first 12 months or by arrangement. There is so much to learn and make decisions about, so an encouraging voice and helping hand are welcome when given generously and kindly. Church planters should honour those who have sent them and express gratitude and share stories to encourage the sending congregations. The more they hear, the more they'll want to do it again.

- **For the church plant team** – Keep the leaders and core team regularly up to date with progress and direction. Challenges are equally important to share so that the burden of leadership is not overly heavy. When a church comes through difficult times together, it binds it together into a strong community of love and fellowship.

STAYING CONNECTED

I believe it is good for newly planted churches to be connected to others. It is too easy to become independently minded to such an extent that you cannot work with others or see the role God has called you to play in the wider Church. When St Paul writes his letters to churches, he is not writing to a single house church but rather collections of churches meeting in a city or region. I find it fascinating trying to work out who is greeted at the end of Paul's letters and what clues these give to how and where they met. But it is clear that Paul expected the various house churches to be united in listening and responding to his instructions and guidance. So consider how you as a church plant can stay connected to the sending church and wider Church. In the Church of England, this includes deaneries which are geographical groupings of churches, but also includes networks of like-minded, theologically aligned churches too.

I benefited hugely by being connected both to a deanery in Tower Hamlets in London as well as being a part of the HTB network of churches.

We learned from others and were able to share with some too; we prayed with many groups and were supported by yet others. We found our place in the wider Church and came to appreciate the unique calling that God had given to us as a church community, as well as recognising that call in other churches near us too.

There are a number of other church networks across the country, including New Wine, National Estates Churches Network, HeartEdge, the Society of Catholic Priests, among others.

Stay connected! It is good for everyone.

A PERSONAL PLEA

All this talk of authority and legalities may seem unspiritual, but it is vital to get it right. Great church plants can come unstuck very quickly without good governance and well-functioning leadership structures and practices. Please pay attention to this as it not only distracts from the mission of the church but also gives church planting a bad name. Take the time as you plan to consider these matters. It will be time well spent.

CALL TO ACTION: AUTHORITY

Use these questions to think through if you have sought the necessary authority for your plant:

- What meetings do you need to put in place with your sending church leader?
- What is your mutually agreed agenda?
- Have you communicated appropriately with the wider church leaders and structures?
- Who are you connected with locally? What can you give and receive from other churches in your area so that all might be enriched and encouraged?
- Are there local governance issues you need to address? (For example, if revitalising an existing church, what is the state of affairs with the PCC?)
- Are you part of a regional or national network of churches that might encourage and support you? How could you join in and play your part in one for mutual benefit?

6

LEADING YOURSELF

HOW TO LEAD A CHURCH PLANT WELL

The health of a church plant is critically dependent on its leader. The leader shapes the culture, sets the pace, oversees the vision, and inspires the team. They lead by example and their character, to some degree, will ultimately be reflected in the church. If you are the leader, it is vital to be honest with yourself. Take a look in the mirror. What's it like to be on the other side of you? What might others not tell you, out of loyalty, politeness, or even fear?

When we planted into Shadwell, I became acutely aware of the requirements of leadership. I had always been in the shadow of other great leaders, but now it felt much more exposing. Who I was began to impact the people I was leading. Flaws quickly became obvious. I realised that it wasn't just the church that needed to survive and thrive, but my family and I needed to as well. The responsibility for enabling that was mine.

As leaders we need to be healthy in every way, self-aware for the sake of others, understanding of what we uniquely, as church planters, are called to do, managing ourselves well, so that we can lead people in the vision that God has given to us. We'll pick up leading others, including the key part our families have to play, in the following chapter.

HEALTH

Healthy church planting leaders are more likely to lead healthy church plants. There are multiple challenges in planting, seen and unforeseen, that make dealing with stress fairly normal. The question though is how we deal with those stresses. Being healthy in multiple dimensions enables us to face these challenges head on without becoming burnt out.

God has made us whole, integrated beings. When one part is over-stretched, it affects other parts too. When I am sick in bed, I find it hard to pray. When I have an unresolved issue with someone, I can't get them out of my mind. When I have too much on my plate, I find it hard to sleep. We must pay attention to the health of every part of ourselves so that we can handle the stresses and strains that inevitably come across our paths. While you cannot separate yourself into independent parts, I find it helpful to think about health in spiritual, emotional, mental, and physical terms, recognising that each will affect the other.

Spiritual health

Spiritual health is about having a good relationship with God and a security in knowing who he has made you to be. In the chapter on Prayer, I addressed the need for the leader and team to foster their dependence on God and following his will. Here I want to look at leading from a spiritually healthy place.

Spiritual health is fostered by lifelong spiritual disciplines that might include meditation, prayer, fasting, study, Scripture reading, sabbath, simplicity, solitude, service, secrecy, sacrifice, submission, confession, worship, fellowship, stewardship, listening, guidance, journalling, witness, and celebration. There's a whole lot there to get your teeth into – hence lifelong! Richard Foster writes, 'The disciplines allow us to place ourselves before God so that he can transform us.'[1] They are developed through daily, weekly, monthly, and annual rhythms, and you need to discern what works best for you.

Early on at university, I was invited to a church where the preacher encouraged anyone who wanted to follow Jesus to give their lives to him. I went forward in response and I was linked up with a man called Kevin who said, 'Let's meet up tomorrow morning at 7 a.m.' I thought this is obviously what Christians all do, so I duly knocked, bleary-eyed, on his door the next morning. We read through 1 John with him asking me questions and inviting me to respond, grounding it in the reality of my life as a student. We did that, verse by verse, every day for three weeks. He taught me to read the Bible, expecting God to speak to me, and he taught me how to apply the Scriptures to my everyday life. He

1 Richard J Foster, *Celebration of Discipline* (London: Hodder & Stoughton, 1989).

taught me how to pray and encouraged me to talk to others about Jesus. He then passed the baton to Tim, one of the friends who had taken me to church. Tim continued meeting with me daily, going through a Bible study booklet called *Every Day with Jesus.* After my first term, 12 weeks later, I had established a practice of getting up early to pray and read the Scriptures, of actively seeking to follow Jesus in every part of my life, of beginning to share my faith with others around me, of joining a small group of other Christians studying the Bible and praying together, and of beginning the first steps of helping someone else to grow in their own discipleship.

We must build regular and resilient spiritual practices that strengthen our faith so that it becomes mature. I have appreciated praying daily with our team, just for 15 minutes on Zoom at the beginning of the working day. I have found writing a journal so helpful when I have needed to process difficult decisions or challenging relationships. Fasting focuses my mind when there are important moments in ministry or when I am needing to see a breakthrough personally. Worshipping on my own deepens my spiritual and emotional connection with God – sometimes I'll even pick up the guitar and sing songs to him. Recently, I took a day to walk across a hill range on my own to pray and spend time in God's presence. These personal practices are all part of building that spiritual resilience.

I am so grateful to the people who helped me get started in my spiritual life, but also to all the leaders and friends who have encouraged me, taught me, and invested in me over the years. But it has always been my responsibility to lean in, to put into practice what I was taught, to strengthen those disciplines so they became a normal routine in my life.

This responsibility is massively helped by inviting others to help you. This is accountability. I have found that accountability is best provided with a number of people and structures, operating in different ways. It is too easy to hide various aspects of our lives from others, so I have to tackle accountability head on and do it honestly and with integrity. Here are the different levels of spiritual accountability at work in my life:

- **Professional** – Keeping up to date with training and checks to ensure I am conducting myself well. For example, annual/semi-annual reviews, Disclosure and Barring Service (DBS) checks, and my responsibilities within church safeguarding dashboards.

- **Fellow leaders** – Attending meetings of peer leaders, where we can choose to be open and honest.

- **Spouses** – If you are married, spouses know us better than most people – warts and all! Loving accountability is a gift.

- **Close friends** – I have been praying regularly with two other friends, Matthew and Greg, since I began training, now for over 30 years. We meet three times a year for 24 hours at a time and are in regular touch outside those times too. We have grown to trust each other deeply and as a result we have given each permission to ask penetrating questions about any area of our lives, including our marriages, what temptations we face, and how we are doing spiritually, emotionally, mentally, and physically. We value the opportunity to 'confess your sins to each other and pray for each other so that you may be healed. The prayer of a righteous person is powerful and effective.'[2] I encourage you to work out what works best for you to help you to be in the best spiritual health you can be.

When we practise accountability ourselves, we can pass it on to others too. Sometimes life is extremely challenging. Storms come and go. Those who invest in their spiritual health, though, are like those who build on rock – when the storms come, you will stand firm,[3] and I assure you, the storms will come!

How are you investing in your own spiritual life? How are you going to ensure that you stick to these rhythms when times are stressful? What do you need to do to continue to grow in spiritual maturity and health?

Emotional health

Emotional health is the ability to manage your moods and feelings. Your spiritual maturity will never grow if you are emotionally immature. If you are easily triggered into anger or sulkiness or depression, if you are defensive when someone criticises you, if you are not able to control strong emotions in moments when others are depending on you, you need to spend time growing healthy emotionally.

2 James 5:16.
3 Matthew 7:24–7.

After a year of our church plant in East London, I found myself thinking that the church was so busy – everyone was exhausted, I was exhausted and almost burnt out, it was all feeling relentless. And I realised that that could only have happened because as a leader I had enabled the level of busyness. I had to take responsibility for my own immaturity and address it both personally and corporately. Our leadership team reflected on this and we decided to do a church-wide deep dive into Peter Scazzero's book, *The Emotionally Healthy Church*. This helped us to look beneath the surface of what we projected, to be prepared to be vulnerable with one another, to recognise our limits, and intentionally to slow down. We also studied John Ortberg's book, *The Life You've Always Wanted*, which took us deeper into spiritual disciplines in a contemporary way.

At a similar time, Louie and I were greatly helped by our friends David and Philippa Stroud, who had led church plants in Bedford and Birmingham, before going on to lead Christchurch London. They encouraged us to make sure we invested in relationships that left us emotionally filled up, especially as we were in leadership roles that were often draining emotionally. We realised that we needed to treat our time off as importantly as our work time, making space for God, for each other, for our children, and for mutually enriching friendships. Similarly, while we chose to open our home to host a number of medium- to long-staying church members, we also realised that hospitality had limits, as we recognised that our children needed space as much as we did.

It is vital to diarise and plan our 'time off'. Sabbath is a command of God, clearly designed for our well-being in every dimension. Working out of rest is very different to resting from work. The former is more challenging to get right but it is more sustainable in the long term. There is a reality about church planting that it is very tiring, and the need to keep a rhythm of rest will benefit our health emotionally as well as physically. We can set an example of taking our days off and taking all our annual leave, making time for recreation, and enriching our lives in ways that may seem less productive in the short term but will reap enormous benefits in the long-term life of the church.

What are healthy rhythms that will help you stay emotionally and relationally strong? What do good boundaries look like for you? What are the limits that you intend to live well within?

Mental health

Mental health is associated with a person's overall mental well-being. It includes rational thinking, good decision-making, and managing difficult situations. Mental health comes from looking after your mind, stretching it like a muscle that needs to be developed, resting it with space and quiet, nurturing it with different experiences, stimulating it with creative moments. There is so much to learn from others and this often comes in the form of books, articles, and podcasts. In Church of England ordinations, deacons, priests, and bishops are all asked, 'Will you be diligent in prayer, in reading Holy Scripture, and in all studies that will deepen your faith and fit you to bear witness to the truth of the gospel?' Studying and learning keep us fresh and alert to growing in our thinking and practice. Good leaders always put themselves in a position of learning – learning best practices, learning for development, learning from mistakes, learning about the culture we are speaking into, learning how to preach effectively, and so on. Leaders are lifelong learners.

Sometimes you need to treat yourself mindfully. My daughter, Zoe, goes for 'mental health walks;' by doing something physical, she addresses a need in her mind. Prayer practices like the Examen, where you work through the day, at the end of the day, before God, can help to process all that has happened in a holistic and prayerful way. As he prepared to plant a church in Bournemouth, Tim Matthews went to a counsellor and said, 'Can we go on a walk together through my emotional landscape and check that no landslides are about to occur? I'd rather that stuff was worked out now rather than a year's time, affecting my wife and family and the congregation.' For me, I need to see a horizon that is further than the buildings right around me in London. It's one of the reasons I regularly make time to go and visit the sea, where the horizon disappears into the distance. It expands my mind and sets the challenges and pressures in a much wider context of the bigness of creation.

I asked Will Van Der Hart at The Mind and Soul Foundation how leaders could maximise their mental health while planting a church. He offered these five excellent tips:

1. Set your personal (and spiritual) priorities before you set your church priorities.

2. Establish your support systems separately from your planting team – accountability, mentorship, supervision, etc.

3. Adopt a 'Retreat to Advance' model using micro-breaks and longer recharging periods over the weeks and months ahead.

4. Listen to your body, and avoid anything that numbs or silences its requests for rest and care.

5. Be honest with yourself about how you feel and be vulnerable with the people who love you.

Physical health

Physical health is the normal functioning of the body. It is about how your body grows, feels, and moves, how you care for it, and what you put into it. My wife Louie is passionate about all aspects of our well-being and she challenges me to get this right, especially in the area of eating, sleeping, and exercising. You need to listen to your body and pay attention to what it is telling you. Someone once said that your body is a major not a minor prophet!

While some people know a lot about eating healthily, some know only a little. With pressurised lifestyles, many people take short cuts in this area, so please pay attention to your diet. If you eat fast-processed food everyday, you will not function at your best. Essential vitamins and nutrients are missing, and unnecessary and unhealthy sugar is added to make it taste better. Young people can get away with eating like this for a while, but it will catch up with you in one way or another, with increasing health problems and lack of resilience to illnesses. When you eat fresh food, have a balanced diet, and drink plenty of water, you are more likely to feel better, be more productive, sleep better, and live longer. This general knowledge is surprisingly ignored by many (especially when life gets busy), but please do your own research to get the best advice.

The missing link to many people's health is not having enough sleep. You need seven to eight hours of sleep per night and you need a good sleep routine. You need to stop looking at computer and phone screens 60 to 90 minutes before sleeping, so you also need a good bedtime routine to help your mind and body get ready for resting. Again, pay attention to caffeine, alcohol, sugar, and processed food intakes because they all affect sleep. Planting often involves lots of evening meetings, so be careful not to self-medicate with chocolate and alcohol! Use mental health practices to allow your mind to process things from the day.

Exercise is essential for physical health. Our bodies function best when our heart rates increase and our muscles are strengthened. With exercise, endorphins are naturally produced in the body that make us feel good. God has designed our bodies to be exercised so, just like a car, our bodies need to go out for a spin. St Paul says that physical exercise is of some value![4] So find a form of exercise you enjoy, otherwise you won't keep it up. You can even combine it with other health habits – an intentional brisk walk every day enables you to pray as well as exercise!

SELF-AWARENESS

You might think that you are healthy in body, mind, and spirit, but you can be unaware of your impact on others – both positively and negatively. If you are gifted in particular ways, it is helpful to be able to develop those gifts so that you can increase their positive impact. If you behave in such a way that is likely to annoy or hurt others, it is good to know about this so you can reduce the negative impacts on others. Self-awareness, especially in leadership, is vital for your own well-being as well as that of your team and those around you.

In England, we are not so good at giving and receiving feedback when it comes to how we lead. Consequently, many leaders never discover how other people experience their leadership, and even if they become aware, they do not make the effort to change for the better. In some church plants, a lack of self-awareness can have difficult and hurtful consequences. In our launch service at St Paul's Shadwell, a member of our team remarked to a local vicar, 'I bet you're really pleased we've come to help sort things out.' The vicar was so offended that he didn't say anything about it to me for two years. In an unguarded moment, he finally revealed the conversation, which helped me understand much of his attitude towards me over those years. I was able to repair some of the relationship, but the harm had been done. Some church planters are so determined to get the job done that there is a trail of destruction behind them in terms of broken relationships and painful experiences. Emotional intelligence works both to see the emotional needs of others as well as how we impact others.

---

4 1 Timothy 4:8.

When we first planted, I found myself winding up my co-leader in ways I could neither see nor understand. I was also frustrated by some of his reactions to some of the situations we faced. We decided we needed help and turned to our friend and leadership expert, Simon Walker. He developed his thoughts on leadership by reflecting on the life and death of Jesus and how we have been formed in childhood and by our backgrounds. His 'Undefended Leadership' model[5] explores seven dimensions of our personalities and how they interact with one another. At its heart, exercising vulnerability and self-emptying, as Jesus did on the cross, is where great leadership leads. In choosing this 'undefended' pathway, we have the freedom to choose the most appropriate leadership style that is best for the particular circumstances rather than being stuck in our own repetitive cycles of behaviour.

Simon's approach to leadership was transformative for us, helping us understand each other and find ways to change our leadership behaviours. It also helped me understand the church we had planted and its place in the wider Church and society, and was both liberating and empowering as a self-reflective leadership tool. I have found other personality models helpful too, both for myself and for the teams I have been a part of or have led, including the Myers-Briggs Type Indicator,[6] the CliftonStrengths assessment[7] (also called Strengths Finder), and Belbin Team Roles.[8]

How well do you know yourself? Do you know the impact you and your behaviour has on others, both positively and negatively? Are you willing to explore this self-understanding more so you can increase your effectiveness as a leader and church planter? Where will you start?

TRAITS OF CHURCH PLANTERS

Are you set up to be a church planter? What kind of person plants churches? What are the attributes or qualities that are often recognised in church planters and pioneers? The bottom line is that many people can plant a church, but those who find themselves drawn or called to this tend to exhibit a number of core indicators.

---

5 Developed in his book, Simon Walker, *The Undefended Leader: Leading out of who you are* (Carlisle: Piquant, 2010).
6 See https://themyersbriggs.com/.
7 See https://www.gallup.com/cliftonstrengths/.
8 See https://www.belbin.com/.

Church planters tend to be leaders who are pioneers; they have ideas for what could be, they generate energy, and create things out of nothing. They are leaders who can gather people around them, and possess a kind of charisma that says, 'Come on, let's go!' and others follow. The church planter needs to have an emotional intelligence that enables them to read a situation and judge the best way of doing what needs to be done, especially important in situations where people can be awkward or difficult. Less favourably, pioneers can sometimes be like a 'bull in a china shop' in their desperation for change to happen, and while they might be great at getting things started, they can sometimes leave a trail of destruction in their path! If you are one of these people, it's good to have someone around you who will kindly make you aware of yourself and keep you accountable. There can be great benefits to seeking counselling at any stage, and particularly before starting a new endeavour, to help you identify problem areas and triggers for your behaviour, and to give you tools to manage.

Church planters are culture setters, determining the culture and atmosphere of the team and of the church. They will need to be optimistic, have a 'can-do' attitude, and be willing to take risks – when necessary!

I have included an expanded list in the appendix which might be useful for building out job descriptions or person specifications, but here are some headline attributes of church planters that we have discerned over the years:

- A natural **starter** with a track record of starting new things.

- A **leader** who casts vision and leads others into this reality, growing leaders to multiply ministry.

- A **gatherer** of people who builds teams.

- A faith **sharer** who communicates the Christian faith naturally to those outside the church and is able to lead them to Christ.

- A **missional** heart with a passion for the extension and growth of God's kingdom.

This list is helpful for self-analysis and merits time for self-reflection from time to time. Ask yourself, how am I doing in these areas? Ask a trustworthy friend or family member who knows you well whether they see these in you. How might you develop these traits in others?

It is always worth remembering that sometimes people who are underrepresented in planting may not see these characteristics in themselves and need others to call them out. They may display these traits outside of traditional church leadership.

TIME MANAGEMENT

A big challenge for church planters is balancing the variety of responsibilities involved in making it happen. Whether you are planting in your spare time, or making initial connections in the community, or launching a larger plant, there is a significant amount of work needed to enable the plant to start up and grow. Time management always seems to be a challenge – or perhaps it's just me?

If you find yourself under pressure in this area, with multiple things to do and always rushing or not delivering as well as you would like to with the time available, I recommend setting apart time to develop this core skill. I have found I need a daily admin process, and certain diarised meetings give me the most space to accommodate the unexpected.

Daily, I use the 'getting things done' process, which is effectively creating a workflow process that you stick to. This one is where you handle an action or a piece of paper only once (I can hear the response: 'In my dreams!'). It's a discipline, but it works for me when I use it!

The second is diarising regular meetings, especially creating more strategic ones: weekly 'day-to-day' planning and review meetings, as well as monthly 'strategic/creative' meetings. I also think it is helpful having full or half days that have no agenda but simply involve listening and giving space for the really meaty items that don't fit into the more regular meetings. If administration is not your natural skill set, you may also want to recruit someone for the team who is detail-oriented and who will love to bring some structure and organisation to your diary. Make sure you support them, and value their input by sticking to their processes as much as possible.

Finally, I try as hard as I can to not take on the wrong burdens. In life, and especially in the Church of England, you are always asked to take on more and more responsibilities. These are often good and valuable tasks, however, we only have so much time and energy to give before we begin to burn out, and our relationships suffer. I strongly recommend accepting only those things which God has clearly called you to do, and saying no to things which he has not, however good they may be.

Jesus guarded his time, ensuring he spent significant time in prayer, time with people, and space to respond to the unexpected. To be like Jesus, perhaps we need to build in a little margin to our diaries so we can lead well in every circumstance.

LEADING THE VISION

The leader embodies the vision and values of the church.

The best leadership that I've seen and experienced combines audacious faith, generosity of spirit, missional zeal, humility, submission to God, blessing of other leaders, and a sense of fun. An emphasis on team, and on unity between churches, demonstrates a humble recognition that you are playing your part among other leaders. These leaders possess a resolve to never give up, and to keep going. Church planting is hard work, and the leader needs to be someone who can rally the troops when the chips are down; to encourage everyone to get up, dust themselves off, and press on! I recommend checking in with yourself and asking, how am I leading the vision? Am I being consistent with our values?

Leadership requires great courage. When I was commissioned by Sandy Millar before we planted to Shadwell, he prayed over us the words of Moses to Joshua: 'Be strong and courageous. Do not be afraid; do not be discouraged, for the Lord your God will be with you wherever you go.'[9] He knew that we would need the courage to go ahead of others, to take steps into the unknown.

Church planters will inevitably go to places where people haven't been before. They are called by Jesus to be vulnerable leaders who serve others. They recognise that they are flawed and are able to make their weaknesses and failures a strength. Character and resilience are required. There are many things to juggle and decisions to be made. Leadership calls must be made on a regular basis, sometimes with little information to hand. The church leader must demonstrate patience, perseverance, and prayerfulness, and a dependence on God rather than their own skill.

9 Joshua 1:9.

Leading others is a continual challenge, and the leader must point those people back to God as their source of strength and sustenance.

FINISHING WELL

We have looked at leading ourselves and ensuring that we are well prepared in every area of our lives – for our own sakes and for the sake of those we are leading. Remember, it is great to start well, with great intentions, but consistency is everything. Leading yourself well is ensuring that you don't fall along the wayside, becoming just another statistic. It is staying the course, with good healthy practices, so that when you finish your race, you can look back on a lifetime of leading well.

CALL TO ACTION: LEADING YOURSELF

- How are you investing in your own spiritual life?
- How does your personal leadership impact others?
- What can you do to improve your health, physically, spiritually, emotionally, and mentally?
- What personal rhythms will you establish to lead well?
- How will you ensure that you stick to these rhythms when times are stressful?

7
LEADING OTHERS

HOW TO BUILD A PLANTING TEAM

It's no surprise that Jesus sent people out in twos. Planting a church alone wouldn't be impossible, but it would be much harder work, with little accountability and support, and perhaps most importantly, it would not model the diversity and breadth of gifts in the body of Christ. Going with others is more fun too, and when one person is down, another can support them with their own gifts and resources – I would advocate having a team of people with you as far as possible!

IMPORTANCE OF TEAM

We are called to be part of the body of Christ, not to go it alone. Leaders in the New Testament were always surrounded by a team. Jesus had a team, including his 12 disciples, and a wider group of others who supported him financially, and accompanied him as he travelled. The apostle Paul was always in a team. On his first missionary journey, he was with Barnabas and Mark. On the second journey, he took Silas then Timothy with him, and they were joined by Luke in Troas. He takes Priscilla and Aquila with him to Ephesus. On the third journey he returned to Ephesus for two to three years, making disciples and training and sending church planters all over Asia Minor (Western Turkey today) so that Luke is able to say 'Asia heard the word of the Lord.'[1] Even in his final days, he called on members of his team to join him: 'Only Luke is with me. Get Mark and bring him with you, because he is helpful to me in my ministry.'[2] The leadership team in the church in Antioch in Acts 13 was made up of prophets and teachers. Paul teaches in 1 Corinthians 12 that we are a body. We need each other, and all have different parts to play.

1 Acts 19:10.
2 2 Timothy 4:11.

In church planting, going on your own can be incredibly lonely and often discouraging. You quickly learn why Jesus sent his disciples out in twos! When we went to St Paul's Shadwell, we not only went with our family, but our friend, Jez Barnes, came with us as associate vicar. We had previously worked together, and in this new season, we encouraged each other, prayed for one another, and wrestled together about the best way to develop and grow the church. We were joined by members of our small group at HTB. Twenty of them moved house across the city, which gave an added sense of being on an adventure together, and it made all the difference in the world.

SUPPORT NETWORK

Everyone's circumstances are different. Church leaders can be single, married with children, or married with none. Some church leaders have chosen the shape of their family life, and others have found themselves in that situation. There is no one correct model for the family life of a church planter. Each brings their own challenges and opportunities.

If you are a single person planting a church, you will need to make sure you have a network of support around you, and safe places and people you can process and be yourself with. Prioritise time with your loved ones, whether it is regular times to talk on the phone or see each other in person. Talk through the joys and difficulties of the planting journey. Ask them to support you in whatever way you need. Go away on holiday with them. Consider scheduling regular time with your small group or group of friends, so that you can receive prayer for yourself and be spiritually supported by that group.

FAMILY

My own experience has come from planting with a 'nuclear family' and, if you have one, they will be the first and most important members of your team. There is a huge range of engagement of spouses and families involved in church planting, and I'm not seeking to suggest there is any one correct way. It will depend on the sense of calling that each person has individually and the couple together in the planting adventure. This range of involvement varies widely and includes spouses co-leading with their partners, leading as part of a leadership team, leading an aspect of ministry but not on the leadership team, supporting as part of a staff team, supporting as a volunteer in the church, supporting as a member but not involved, or maybe not involved at all.

The important thing is to be clear about everyone's expectations, and communicate them.

If you do have a spouse and family, obviously to some extent you are in it together. You will need to fully consider the impact on them. Be honest. How far do they need or want to be involved? Leadership of a church plant is the same as leading a regular church, but, like any start-up, is even more intense. Whatever their role, each member of the family needs to be on board with the plant, and not feel they are competing with it for your attention.

Some will see church planting together as being a 'family on mission,' as we did. While acknowledging and understanding the many pressures, we sought to take our children with us, in every sense. We were all in, wanting to equip our children to face the challenges and opportunities of the mission that God had for them as much as for us. Others will give their children more freedom to be less involved, and it may partly depend on age and personal choice.

I asked my wife and (now adult) children's thoughts on being a church planting family, and these are their reflections:

1. **Clarify your priorities from the outset** – God – marriage – children – mission, in that order. And stick to it! To set aside personal worship and prayer time with our spouse is obviously important, but so often it is the first thing to go when time is tight. Invest in your marriage time. It is important to take your responsibilities seriously. Church leaders can be so emotionally absorbed in pastoring others that they have few resources left for their families.

2. **Focus on the family** – Leaders must remember their family deserves their best attention. The whole family is involved in planting a church. And the health of the church will reflect the health of your own family. Everything flows out of that. Build routines, protect family time, do not compromise on your children's happiness. We were helped by a local church leader who was honest enough to admit that although they put their children into the local school for mission purposes initially, for them, it was a disaster and they

needed to be taken out. That's not right for everyone but it's important not to assume your children will simply adjust. Listen to them – if we're all on mission together. God was preparing our children too. I remember our six-year-old daughter Zoe saying on a car journey: 'When we move I'll make new friends.' We hadn't mentioned moving at that point, but God was assuring her – and us – that he had her best intentions at heart.

3. **Authenticity and integrity are vital** – We all need a safe place to be ourselves. Decide as a family what your special values are, record them, and pray about how you will live them out. Your family is unique and will not look exactly like any other. Know who you are as a family, talk about what your joint calling is and how each of you fulfil a different role in that.

4. **Have fun** – Celebrate anything and everything you can, at home and in the church. Some friends of ours always kept a bottle of bubbly in the fridge, ready to celebrate and rejoice in any event. Keep up with those friendships which are particularly life-giving and be open to making new ones. Give your children a sense of continuity by keeping in touch with old family friends. Plan holidays and fun things in advance to look forward to – put the tickets on the mantelpiece or noticeboard to remind you every day. Keep time aside for hobbies and other play activities.

5. **Set boundaries** – There will always be more to do – but just because it is a good thing to say yes to, does not mean it is the best thing. Are you being fully present with your spouse and family? It's possible to be physically present but emotionally or mentally miles away. Your spouse might be the only one who can gently point this out – try not to be defensive! We practise the 10 p.m. rule – no serious conversations after that as they are usually completely unproductive! Lack of boundary-keeping can lead to mistrust and resentment – one leader's wife informed her husband that she was so frustrated, she was leaving the church. That stopped the leader in his tracks and helped him to start listening to her. Be honest, and be releasing of your older children, allowing them to be less involved if they wish. Watch

for signs of stress in them and react accordingly. Keep an eye on their physical as well as spiritual well-being. Our bodies might show the signs before we notice other things. Have a support network – we wouldn't have survived without our small group. Well-being is essential.

6. **Don't let the enemy get a foothold** – He wants you to fail (and you will at times), but remember that God has the victory. Changing seasons and (hopefully) church growth means you will need to regularly check in on your patterns for marriage time, family routines, everything. Does anything need adjusting? Bring it back to worship. Pray for each other.

7. **Have a reset button** – If things don't work out, don't throw it all out, just push the reset button and start again. God's mercies are new every morning! Rhythms help for fresh starts – a new day, a new week, a new term, a new year. There will be times when there are major issues in the church, and you won't always get it right. We were once so overwhelmed with a relational problem in the church that it deeply affected our family and our marriage. The intensity of that time overshadowed every part of our lives and it took months to resolve. In the midst of this intense time, we needed to give space for each other and we needed lots of God's grace, which he always provides.

RECRUITING

Your family may have had no choice but to be on your team – but others do! How do you decide who to recruit to your team? I think there is a difference between the core team and the wider team. The core team might be the beginnings of a leadership team. They are people who would sacrifice much to be part of this adventure with you and they will go out of their way to serve and support the vision. The wider team might be less committed than that but still up for joining you. As you pray, the people God is calling will step forward, and if there is a clear way of expressing an interest, you can mutually discern if it is the right step. I find myself using the Cs of recruitment more and more, whether for teams or for staff, and it is worth using this as a framework for talking to potential team members:

- **Calling**: How do you feel God is calling you to join this plant?

- **Courage**: Are you willing to throw yourself into the vision?

- **Culture**: Do you get the values of our plant and the way we hope to do things?

- **Character**: Do you have the strength to stand through the challenges and storms?

- **Competence**: How could you serve the plant with your passions and skills?

- **Chemistry**: Could we get along and laugh together? Could we be honest with each other?

- **Consistency**: Do you have the resilience necessary for what lies ahead?

We are definitely not seeking perfection, but the above questions might give you a sense of the kind of people who are stepping forwards. There might be some people who are not ready or perhaps where you feel it won't work and you need to find a way of gently saying 'no,' or 'not for now.' The apostle Paul had to say no to Barnabas about Mark joining the team on their second mission trip and it was difficult at the time – they had a sharp disagreement and parted ways! But we see later that Paul says of Mark that he is useful to him. He wasn't ready before but he has learned much and things changed. Recruit wisely!

However, context plays a big part in how planters go about recruiting a team. Things may look very different from plant to plant. Archdeacon Sally Gaze uses a cooking analogy when describing the differences there can be in building a team for a well resourced urban parish or in the countryside. She says:

> I would say that urban planting is like 'cooking from the recipe book' in that you usually have an idea of what you are aiming for and can get the ingredients you need to make the meal. With rural planting, it feels like you are 'cooking from the fridge' – you may have a chocolate bar, an aubergine and an onion – and you've got to make a meal! In other words, in less populated areas, you don't necessarily have all the people with the gifts you'll need. But God knows what you need. So I would say, let's design around what God has given us; ask, 'Who has God given me? Who is he calling?' Work with those people, having faith that he knows what he is doing.

Sally describes how she has sometimes been surprised by people who have come forward, seemingly from nowhere, including a retired farmer who asked to have a chat with her. 'He told me he was a licensed evangelist and had a heart for the farming community – could we use him? He is now a Lightwave rural chaplain and out of that conversation, a whole agricultural ministry has been born.'

SETTING TEAM EXPECTATIONS

One of the questions which often comes up is, what is the team signing up for? When we announced our plant, we invited anyone who wanted to be on the team with us to sign up. The vision was the compelling narrative for joining in, but we didn't give them many specific details. With only a month to go, we started working with those on the list to plan the launch and the first few months of the plant. We seemed to think we would just muddle through! In hindsight, we should have been more focused and intentional about expectations so that everyone knew what the core commitments were.

Working with many plants since then, I now encourage five simple commitments expected from being a member of a planting team:

1. **Belong** – Make this plant your church, rather than going back to the sending church. Throw yourself fully into belonging to the plant. You could agree on a timescale that the planting team commits to, for example, two years. This helps volunteers know that it's not a time away for a few weeks but rather a length of time that will make a difference and get some momentum going.

2. **Serve** – Throw yourself into serving in a particular way, whether it is helping with communications, welcoming, refreshments, music, etc. Play your part and make serving part of the culture.

3. **Pray** – Pray for the church plant and its leaders, but also ensure that your own prayer life is on track. The assumption is that each member of the team, where possible, will join whenever the church meets for prayer.

4. **Give** – Give financially to the church plant. Move your giving from your sending church to the new church. If you are not used to giving a proportion of your income in a planned way, this is a

great time to start. Financial giving is a mark of discipleship and getting this right will set you free from the fear of not having enough.

5. **Disciple** – Jesus' command to 'Go and make disciples' is for everyone. Who will you help to grow in their faith? Who will step up to lead a small group? Who will be intentional about helping someone else to grow personally?

I show people the five commitments on the fingers of my hand when I explain it so people can remember it and they know what to aim for. When the team is doing these things, they are effectively setting the culture of the church so that new people joining the church community catch this culture and start doing it themselves. These are caught much more easily than being taught, but teaching them will reinforce it in the life of your church.

TEAM GIFTS AND DYNAMICS

I keep emphasising that we are not called to lead alone. In the Church of England, my training equipped me to be able to do everything well; to lead a church, to preach and to teach, to pastor and care, to pray and to evangelise, to start new projects, and to administrate. Yet I found that I was only middling at some of those things, and useless at others. It doesn't take long when reading the Scriptures to realise that we are not called to be an expert on everything, but to be someone who looks at the gifts that God has given us, and given others, and to utilise those, to be the body of Christ. St Paul says that some have been given the gift of leadership, others the gift of healing, and his letter to the Corinthians tells us that we are not supposed to do everything alone. Ephesians 4 talks about fivefold ministry in equipping the saints for the work of ministry. We thrive when we look to each other, rather than just looking within ourselves for ability and strength. A self-aware leader can bring others onto the team who have different gifts to them, to complement them and the team. A really secure leader will celebrate that someone on the team is more gifted in a certain area than they are!

Bernice Hardie discovered the importance of building a team whose gifts complement yours. She started WAVE Church (We're All Valued

Equally), an inclusive worshipping community for people with and without learning disabilities, when she couldn't find an inclusive worship setting for her own daughter to join. As a lay planter, Bernice admits that she had 'no experience of church leadership so relied on having a supportive team around her from the very start.' Her team made all the difference to being able to carry on or not at the beginning. Many of them had family members with learning disabilities or some professional connection. Bernice says:

> It has been amazing how God has brought along all the people we need. We were very lucky at the outset to have an SEN (Special Educational Needs) teacher who had run a Messy Church so had some really practical skills and ensured we had safeguarding elements in place. We have people who are good at tech, and a very talented musician to lead our music and we've got people like Sally, Christiane and Jane, who provide tea and cake and clear up. They do all the washing up and are always the last to leave. Then there are the people who pray, like Maureen, an older lady who was an absolute prayer warrior when we started. I think she kept me sane in those first couple of years.[3]

There might be someone on your team, the leader perhaps, who is great at evangelism and making a lot of connections but would naturally look to others to pastor people. This highlights the need to have someone with pastoral strengths on your team. Someone else might be a great Bible teacher, hugely valuable to teach the growing church about the depths of the Christian faith. There might be prophetic people who are gifted at hearing God, and always seem to give encouraging or pertinent words at the right time. As it says in 1 Corinthians, 'the one who prophesies speaks to people for their strengthening, encouraging and comfort.'[4] Some will have a special gift of intercession and others will prophetically call the team to prayer, and listen to what God is saying. The point here is that there are many types of gifts, including administration and working with families, and we need to use them all. If you want something to grow, you need others to help.

---

3 A story from *Send Me: Stories of ordinary people planting new churches*, edited by John McGinley (London: CCX, 2023).
4 1 Corinthians 14:3.

DELEGATION

It is tempting for the plant leader to try to do everything themselves. However, this is bound to lead to burn-out for the leader and frustration for all those around them. It's important to have a team mentality, where the team leader gives roles away rather than trying to do it all. This means delegating in all areas of the life of the church: setting up, in hospitality and welcome, in missional outreach projects, in setting down.

Be mindful as you gather a team, and ask yourself, 'Who needs to be drawn in?' The kind of team you need is twofold. Firstly, you need to be able to fit functionally. It wouldn't be ideal to have five worship leaders and no one else. Think about a spread of functions that would enable you to work together, where people can take on different responsibilities in light of their different gifts and skill sets. Secondly, friendship is important. When the battles are raging, it's so good being in relationships where you can spur one another on, and laugh and cry together. This is more difficult when you don't know the person you are working with, or where there might not be that natural chemistry. Having said that, if a team is all the same, you are going to end up leading a church made of people who are very similar. This isn't much of a reflection of the picture in Galatians 3:28 – we are 'all one in Christ Jesus' – there is a real sense of multiplicity of people and types. As with all things, it's important to strike a balance. You might decide to set out on a plant with a friend initially, and as the church grows you will need to recruit for other specific roles. Church planting demands a kind of friendship where you can speak and hear the truth with and from others, and where there is mutual trust. This is harder in a purely functional relationship and takes work.

DEVELOPING ROLES

The roles on a church planting team will depend entirely on the vision for that plant, and the stage it is at. Obviously, a small team planting a community in a café will not require an operations manager or a director of music. A team going in to revitalise a parish may require a larger team from the outset, with a worship leader and a children's worker. A small team may work voluntarily for some time before an eventual permanent staff team is established. In the case of smaller church communities, a small team can cover all of these roles on a voluntary basis, even in the long term.

Different church plants have different financial circumstances. The important question to work out is, do you pay any of your team? The first thing to say is that the role itself is more important than employment. Work out what you need first of all. There might be people in the congregation who could do the roles in their own time, although if you are able to pay for people, those areas of ministry will usually grow faster, as more time and energy can be put into the work. A judgement call needs to be made about whether the roles will be voluntary or paid, full-time or part-time. My encouragement is to think about covering all of these roles in whatever way is possible for your plant.

Your team could include the following roles, which may develop over the course of the church plant:

- **Church plant leader** – There will be different seasons in the life of the church plant which call for different styles of leadership. The skills required to start a church plant from scratch, inspire, and build a team (see traits of church planters in chapter 6) are different to when the church is developed and moving into an established phase. It's wise to reassess after the first few years, to see if you are still the right person to lead the plant. I know one person who was like a serial planter. They moved on every four or five years because they were great at starting things but recognised that they needed to pass the leadership on to someone with different skills to take the church on to the next stage in its development.

- **Assistant leader** – To help the leader by increasing capacity and freeing up him or her to focus their energies on different things. This assistant leader also provides a reflective place for the leader to be able to talk through things in confidence. The effect is also to double the capacity for pastoral oversight and add to the potential for growth of different ministries. The assistant leader, for example, might take responsibility for the midweek groups in church, or developing social transformation ministries, allowing the leader to concentrate on other areas of ministry or team development. The assistant leader is effectively an apprentice, learning how to plant a church. Perhaps in time, after one to three years, that person will go on to lead their own church plant, and you should be clear in setting expectations and communicating with them about this possibility as time goes on. In appointing an assistant, or apprentice, you are enabling the capacity of the church plant to continue planting. You will be planting a church-planting church! Last, but not least, when the primary leader goes on holiday or takes a break, they will be able to leave the running of the church in the hands of the assistant.

- **Worship leader/director of music** – To oversee and lead worship, depending on the type of church and the vision. If the church has a vision for running large attractional services, it may need to recruit excellent worship leaders. The plant may choose to invest in music from the outset as an important feature of their ministry, and to develop new music as a resource and gift to the wider Church. In churches where music is important but not as prominent, decent musicians are required in order to enable services. Other plants may focus on a 'everyone can join in' style, where inclusion is key and no one minds too much about it being at a professional level. Of course, it is possible to have a church without a worship leader, or without a musician leading. But it is ideal to have some live music, and the quality of music as a church grows becomes important.

- **Operations manager** – Any gathering of people requires some degree of administrative support to facilitate clear communication and smooth functioning of the life of the church. This is a skilled and vital role, and will need to be reassessed regularly as priorities change and the church grows. Some purely administrative tasks can be delegated, such as managing the database of members, overseeing communications, running the day-to-day finances of the church, and human resources requirements such as contracts, payroll, and producing job descriptions. If the church is based in a building, there will be additional tasks in terms of site management and maintenance. Then there will be the running of events, just one of which will be the Sunday service. These might be coordinated by one person, or split up between a number of people, depending on how the team is run.

- **Safeguarding officer** – This is a vital role, for which they will need training. (For more detail on this key topic see the following chapter on Resources.)

- **Children's leader and youth worker** – When families join a church, the parents are seeking discipleship for their children as much as for themselves. If you want to see your church grow, or if there are already a large number of children you want to minister to, having a children's worker is key. There are a number of challenges when it comes to church planting and children, one of which is looking after both churched and unchurched children, presenting different mission opportunities. The second challenge comes when trying to anticipate the age groups of the children you might be ministering to. When we went to St Paul's Shadwell there were three children – our own! They were six, four, and two, and a friend began to look after them on Sundays as Louie and I led the services. As other people in the church started having children, and as other families began to join, we needed to develop a team of children's helpers. At first this was coordinated by one person, and then after a few years we recruited a professional children's worker. This is when children's work at the church really took off. Some church plants recruit professional children's or youth workers to take the opportunity to go into local schools and run after-school clubs. There is a key challenge when children reach the age of around 11, when they are moving on to secondary school, and parents are reflecting on whether their church is meeting the needs of the child. Getting a youth worker to run the growing youth work can create a hub for young people, not just for one church plant but for other churches in the area.

Finally, it is pragmatic to accept that people's circumstances change, and they may not be able to continue on the team as long as you or they would wish, for whatever reason. End well – thank them, release them, and celebrate their sacrifice and service.

TEAM SIZE

It is also worth considering how big your planting team should be at each stage. I think that ours was too big when we planted into St Paul's Shadwell. Twenty people from our home group moved church and joined the team; one family sold their property and bought a flat local to the church. There were 80 people who already lived in East London and who had been travelling across London to our church. They joined us too.

Starting with 100 people, with about 70 attending at any one time, was wonderful on the one hand – we had lots of momentum and people to help get ministries started – but on the other hand, it felt like big church already with an expectation of the provision of ministries that they had from the sending church. Equally, a planting team can also be too small to build up critical mass and capacity. You need enough people to give the sense that something exciting is happening, which draws in other people, and to run the ministry in that place. In a revitalisation of a parish church, a large incoming team might be needed to get things going. Or a large team might overwhelm the existing congregation. In a smaller planting situation, a small team might be best because they can pay the right attention to listening and adapting to that specific context.

The size of your team requires careful thought, although 'who' is more important than 'how many.' With years of planting experience behind him, Archie Coates says he's realised while you can't plant without people, there's more to it than raw numbers: 'You can plant with only a handful of people, so long as they are the right handful.'

LEADERSHIP DEVELOPMENT

A key part of developing the church planting team will be to develop the leadership potential of each person on the team. I have learned that leadership development requires a significant amount of investment, but it has a disproportionately positive impact on what you are trying to do and the long-term legacy you leave behind. If you make time for developing others from day one, it will never feel like an extra, but rather just a part of what you do. It is both an individual practice and a collective system. I have met many people who say they don't have any leaders in their church and so they are limited in what they can do. I respond by saying, you might not have any mature leaders, but you have a lot of undeveloped leaders, waiting to be invested in, trained, developed, and deployed. I would encourage all church planters to do what Jesus did and start developing future leaders from the very beginning.

This starts with setting the culture. The leader will always define the culture, either intentionally or accidentally, so how do you create a healthy culture in a church plant where all the team are encouraged to be the best they can be? Most leaders lead their team in a way that they would like to be led – but that is not always how the team member may respond best. Start by becoming more self-aware, and then get to know each team member. Using the Support/Challenge matrix tool may help.

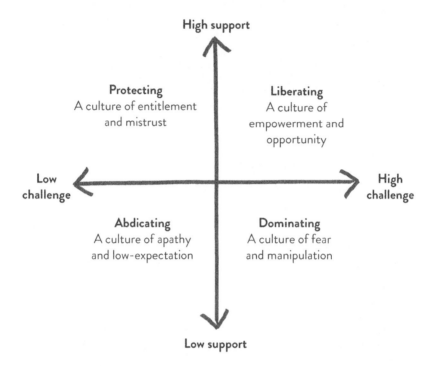

Figure 13: The Support/Challenge matrix (Property of GiANT Worldwide)

Jesus modelled **liberating** leadership with his team, and this is the standard we should aim for in both our work and personal relationships. The Support/Challenge matrix visually defines this standard and helps us make it a reality in our own lives. It requires us to bring high support and high challenge to those we lead and love. That is how we create a culture of empowerment and opportunity that leads to high performance.

The problem is that most of us are not naturally liberating leaders! Some of us bring a lot of challenge, and struggle to match it with the same level of support. Over time this creates a culture of fear and manipulation as people experience us as **dominating** them. Other leaders are highly relational and always bring high support, willingly going the extra mile to serve and care for those they lead. Their difficulty might be in bringing the level of challenge that matches their high support. When you over-support and under-challenge in an effort to **protect** relational harmony, you create a culture of entitlement, and eventually mistrust, when passive aggression can even turn into anger. Finally, burnt-out leaders or those who have given up offer neither high support nor high challenge. They abdicate their responsibility to lead and create a culture of apathy and low expectations. The Support/Challenge matrix is a simple way to assess your own leadership in relation to Jesus'; it helps you understand what it's really like to be on the other side of your leadership and shows clearly what growth is needed for you to be experienced as a liberating leader, creating a culture of empowerment and opportunity.

Having set the culture, what other tools will you use? If you are the plant leader, you can choose individuals to invest in, maybe an assistant leader or someone who you think has leadership potential. This is best discerned in prayer and by asking if that person would be interested in taking on more leadership responsibility. This might happen over a period of time, but it can happen in every context you have – leading services, preaching, leading ministries, small groups, and events. It is helpful to start small and grow opportunities to develop them. The most important input is yourself and your time. Then whenever leadership opportunities arise, give them the chance to have a go. The leadership square tool on the next page will help you develop the person at each stage of their learning.

THE LEADERSHIP SQUARE

I have found the leadership square, among others, a really useful tool to have in mind as you help to grow each of your team. It follows the stages of: 'I do, you watch;' 'I do, you help;' 'you do, I help;' 'you do, I watch;' gradually giving more and more opportunity and responsibility to those you are investing in. When they are ready, encourage them to do the same for someone else: 'you do, someone else watches.' Each stage involves a different posture – envisioning, coaching, shared leadership, and delegation. I use it to discern where a leader is in their development and how best to move them to the next stage.

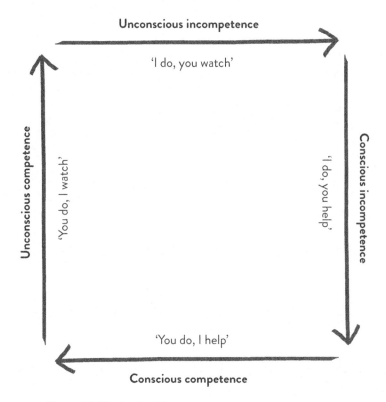

Figure 14: The leadership square (Property of GiANT Worldwide)

This model is often used in management circles, but I notice these four stages of leadership in Jesus' ministry too. The first stage is a clear and simple call: Jesus said to his disciples, 'Come, follow me,' not asking for their opinions but instead inviting them to 'look at what I do.' This exciting stage in the disciple's journey is 'unconscious incompetence.' They don't know what they don't yet know! With the disciples ministering to the crowds alongside Jesus, they don't yet realise that they don't know what they are doing, and they are filled with enthusiasm for the cause.

The second stage is 'conscious incompetence.' The disciples become aware of how hard the job is, and Jesus has to call them away to spend time with him. The leader's role here is to keep the direction going, and to model how to lead and minister well. There is a need for increased time here, for encouragement, for discussion and reflection. Before, in the first stage, there wasn't a huge amount of time because the disciples were encouraged to follow and join in with what Jesus was doing. The second stage is about quality time, and moving towards a coaching style of leadership. Jesus gives his disciples time, vision, and grace; reminding them that it's not about them, it's about the kingdom. It is at this stage that the disciples, and indeed whomever you are leading, have the realisation that they are not very experienced and there is much room for improvement. This stage can be painful (it's the pit of despair in one graphic!) and the leader will need to keep talking about the vision to re-inspire the team when needed.

Hudson Taylor, a missionary to China in the 19th century, said that there were three stages to mission: first it's impossible, then it is difficult, and then it is finished – or you are finished! There comes a time when the journey becomes very challenging, and leadership at this stage is crucial. There is a need to spend time with those you are leading, to keep giving vision and reminding them of God's grace. Vision driving grace, and grace driving vision. Having gone from the first stage of visionary leadership, you now enter into consensus, or a coaching-oriented leadership. One of the most difficult things as the leader is to help move people around the next corner of the square.

The third stage is 'conscious competence.' The disciples here are doing things, and they are working, but it still may not come naturally, and they are conscious of every move. At this stage, Jesus says to them, in John 15:15, that they are no longer servants but friends. In this third stage of leadership, there is a move from a kingdom focus to a much stronger covenant focus, built on friendship and relationship. This is often a time of growth for a team, and for the disciples, was the start of increasing revelation. They become more aware of what is going on and grow in confidence. They have pulled through the difficulties of the second stage, and are beginning to see the sick healed, demons cast out, and are getting more involved themselves. Here there is a leadership change; Jesus calls them friends, rather than just followers. There is a higher level of detail here, and there are hints of Jesus' departure, as he is preparing them for when he is gone.

The fourth and final stage is 'unconscious competence.' The disciples are growing in confidence and do not need as much direction. Jesus is letting them make their own decisions and doesn't give much explanation. The resurrected Jesus is sometimes present, and often not. The disciples understand that Jesus is with them, even though he is not visibly there all the time. This is a delegating leadership style. The disciples are ordinary people when Jesus began to lead them, but they were extraordinary when he finished.

There are so many ways to train and develop leaders, once you have identified those who might have leadership potential or who are already leading others. There is apprenticeship, where every existing leader takes one or two apprentices and develops them in a systematic way using tools such as the leadership square; running courses on specific topics in groups; one-to-one training with a more senior leader; peer groups of leaders learning together; self-learning (reading, studying, etc), and of course on-the-job, which accounts for most learning.

LEADERSHIP PIPELINE

We've looked at identifying gifts in people, developing their leadership skills, and delegating well. As mission and ministry grows, more people will need to become leaders and they will need to be trained and developed. How can we develop a flow of leaders in the right positions at the right time who are ready to play their part in the church?

In 2 Timothy 2:2, Paul talks about a number of stages of leadership when he is writing to Timothy about developing his oversight: 'And the things you have heard me say in the presence of many witnesses entrust to reliable people who will also be qualified to teach others.' In Paul's mind, he is equipping Timothy to train 'reliable people able to teach,' who in turn will teach others. This is four generations of leaders, and might give us a framework for thinking about organising leaders today.

Translating this into a church context today, many people are using the idea of a leadership pipeline which imagines different levels of leaders, leading in different ways, and developing them. Taking Paul's four generations of leader, we can add a fifth of leading ourselves, because that involves everyone, including those being led. Church members might well be involved in leading others in other spheres of life, but I am using it with regard to ministry roles. This might look like the following:

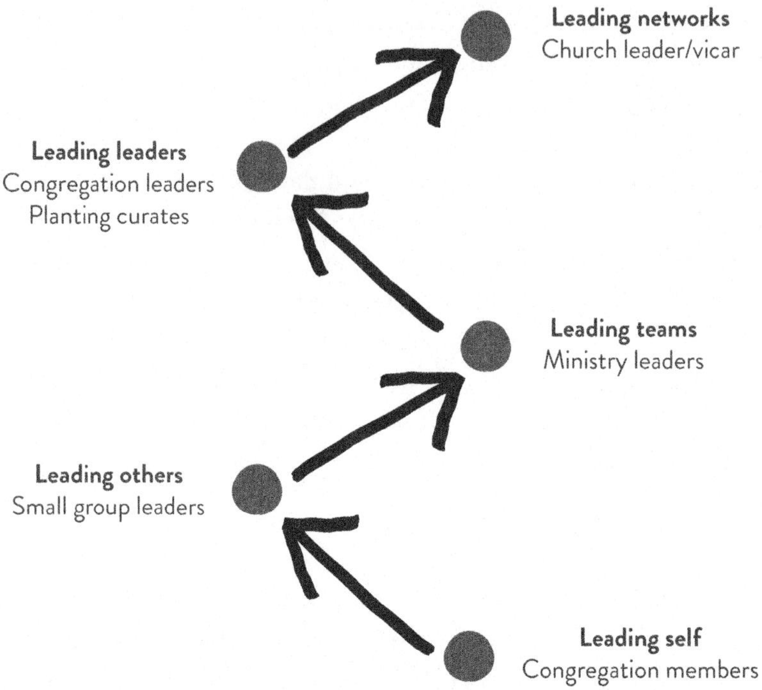

Leading networks
Church leader/vicar

Leading leaders
Congregation leaders
Planting curates

Leading teams
Ministry leaders

Leading others
Small group leaders

Leading self
Congregation members

Figure 15: The leadership pipeline

The leadership pipeline will look different for each church and church plant, but the different stages may include leading self, leading others, leading teams, leading leaders, and leading networks of leaders. I have added some roles above to show what it looked like in our church plant. I worked out all the leadership needs, then added the leaders we already had to those roles, and that left a number of leadership gaps that we knew needed filling. That then showed us who we needed to identify, and how we needed to train them up and give them opportunities to step up into those leadership roles. To start with, we didn't have enough leaders, but within a couple of years, we were overflowing with leaders ready to move up to the next level of leadership. This meant we always had leaders ready to go out on the next plant without depleting our existing needs.

Using Paul's encouragement to Timothy, we can apply this to the leadership pipeline in terms of developing each leader at their particular stage. Paul was looking for people of good character ('reliable') and who are growing in their skills ('qualified to teach'). Any development of leaders should then be about equipping them to grow in character and to grow in skill.

People grow in their skills through training and apprenticeship, which I talk about in the next chapter. More importantly, we can help people grow in their character by teaching them about what Jesus calls us to be like, about a lifestyle and behaviour outlined, for example, by St Paul in the first chapter of Titus. D. L. Moody famously said that our character is what we are like in the dark! We might ask ourselves, what needs to change? How can I grow in these areas of Christian character?

INTENTION IS EVERYTHING

Building, developing, and leading your team is absolutely essential in the adventure of planting a church. It will bring joys and challenges in equal measure, and it may take longer than we might like it to. But long term, having a pipeline of developing leaders, with a healthy culture, will not only benefit your church plant but the growth of the whole Church, now and into the future.

CALL TO ACTION: LEADING OTHERS

Think through these questions to help you plan how you'll build your team:

- What's the most appropriate team for the church you are planting?
- Does anyone need to be paid at this point?
- How will you balance team roles and existing friendships?
- What role will your family play in your plant? Have you spoken about your mutual expectations? And, how will you help them to flourish in the plant?
- What gifts do you need to bring onto your team to complement yours?

8
RESOURCES

HOW TO SET UP YOUR PLANT OPERATIONALLY

Our most important resource is the Holy Spirit. Remembering this, we are free to plan our structures, finances, measurement, reporting, training, communications, IT, and all the other systems we need to enable the church to work and run well. Without him, there is no proper church, and we need to keep asking for more of his presence and power and all the resources he generously provides. We are dependent on the Lord for these resources and we are called to steward them well.

Let's start with ensuring we have a safe church.

SAFEGUARDING

Safeguarding is far and away the most important part of setting up good operations. It is one of the ways we follow the gospel imperative to protect and care for the most vulnerable in our communities. The Church of England is committed to safeguarding as an integral part of its ministry and mission, promoting a safer culture and the welfare of every child, young person, and adult. It is therefore an essential foundation for church planters to build so that their church is a safe place for all, and so safeguarding needs resourcing. The best place to start is to contact your local safeguarding representative; within the Church of England this will be the Diocesan Safeguarding Officer. Safeguarding policies may vary somewhat across denominations, but in the Church of England all who are licensed to minister have a duty to follow nationally approved guidance and codes of practice. These are readily available online and from diocesan safeguarding officers. Spend time with them to ensure that safeguarding is addressed as part of your planting process.

There will need to be robust policies, procedures, and guidelines in place to ensure good practice throughout all that you are doing. Safeguarding is not a tick-box exercise, it is about genuinely creating and maintaining a safe environment and culture, where everyone will be motivated and empowered to look out for the safety of all. This kind of culture will mean that harm is prevented, that any concerns or allegations are responded to promptly, and that victims and survivors of abuse and other affected persons are cared for pastorally. To promote this culture you will want to ensure the following things are in place:[1]

- A leadership commitment, at all levels, to the importance of safeguarding and promoting the welfare of children, young people, and vulnerable adults.
- A safeguarding policy available to church officers.
- A clear line of accountability within the Church for work on safeguarding.
- Clear reporting procedures to deal with safeguarding concerns and allegations.
- Clear roles for church officers.
- Practice and services informed by ongoing learning, review, and by the views of children, young people, families, and vulnerable adults.
- Safer recruitment procedures in place.
- Clear arrangements for support and/or supervision.
- Safeguarding training for all church officers working with or in contact with children, young people, and/or vulnerable adults.
- Effective working with statutory and voluntary sector partners.
- Publicly advertised arrangements for children, young people, and vulnerable adults to be able to speak to an independent person, as required.
- Complaints and whistleblowing procedures that are well publicised.
- Effective information sharing.
- Good record keeping.

Church plants attract new members and we need to have structures in place to care pastorally for any who might be the subject of concerns or allegations of abuse and other affected persons, as well as responding

1 https://www.churchofengland.org/sites/default/files/2019-05/PromotingSaferChurchWeb.pdf.

quickly to those that may pose a present risk to others. It is always important to consult with your diocesan safeguarding officer if any member of your plant is an ex-offender.

Depending on your context, following proper safeguarding procedures can sometimes be complex. Mary Hervé pioneered a worshipping community that serves ex-offenders in Guernsey, called Thursday Church. It began when some ex-offenders attended an Alpha course at her church and wanted to continue to meet as a small group. This group became a congregation in its own right, meeting with a core of others from her church. Mary recognised that safeguarding was a complex issue for them. Everyone who goes to Thursday Church knows that there are ex-offenders in the group, but doesn't necessarily know who they are, or the nature of their crimes. To be safeguarding compliant, she works very closely with statutory agencies, the police, the probation service, Employment and Social Security Department, offender management, mental health services, and third sector organisations. They are part of the MAPPA team – Multi Agency Public Protection Arrangement. She says that her main safeguarding supports are the police and probation service and the diocesan safeguarding lead. By following these procedures, she keeps everyone in her church safe.[2]

The Church of England uses 'parish safeguarding dashboards' that outline the training, policies, procedures, and guidelines that need to be worked through. Make sure you allocate time to work through these as a team and appoint someone on the team to be the church safeguarding officer so that they are able to ensure everything is in place. See the Church of England safeguarding page on their website for access to all their resources.[3]

EMPLOYING STAFF

Many churches and church plants struggle to follow appropriate human resources procedures: posts are not always advertised and staff are not always properly supervised. When we do this, we are treating our staff unfairly, and not giving them the right conditions to flourish. It is so important that we value people, and deal with them professionally and kindly. Good human resources procedures are one of the ways that we can

2 A story from *Send Me: Stories of ordinary people planting new churches*, edited by John McGinley (London: CCX, 2023).
3 www.churchofengland.org/safeguarding.

do this, because it helps to give people a workplace they can thrive in. If you have any questions, contact your diocese's Employment and Human Resources department who may be able to offer you advice.

FINANCES

Faith and finances go together in church planting, but it is unwise to start planning to spend lots of money if you don't have it in the bank! Jesus tells a parable related to this in the context of the cost of following him. He says, 'Suppose one of you wants to build a tower. Won't you first sit down and estimate the cost to see if you have enough money to complete it? For if you lay the foundation and are not able to finish it, everyone who sees it will ridicule you, saying, "This person began to build and wasn't able to finish."'[4]

You will need to carefully balance what God is calling you to do, estimating how much it is going to cost, and working out how the money will arrive in your account. There are no right answers to the 'how.' It might be through an unexpected gift from an unknown source, or from someone you ask directly, or from the generous offerings of the congregation who are sending you. So let's explore this a little more.

Money helps

There are a number of models that are relatively low cost and this is the main way that church planting happens around the world. Following the New Testament model in Acts, churches were planted in people's homes so there was no rent or building works to consider. Parking obviously wasn't an issue! The only costs went to supporting the poor or towards enabling apostolic ministry, releasing leaders to work part- or full-time for the church. In many places, churches are still planted in people's homes and the costs are low if not free. Some churches meet outdoors or in free public venues. For example, Forest Church in Weston-super-Mare began when a group began to gather at a community allotment. They eventually decided to begin a Sunday afternoon gathering (now held fortnightly on Saturdays), based around their experience of God in nature. Their first gathering had 25 people from the village, all unchurched, and have had

4 Luke 14:28–30.

up to 68 people some weeks![5] Lambeth Palace and Southwark Diocese planted St Mary's Eco Church in response to the climate emergency and biodiversity crisis. Their vision is to create innovative spaces for people to encounter each other, the rest of nature, and God, celebrating their differences and diversity. They hold their Eucharist outside, and their other gatherings are either in local parks or public venues. For both of these plants, having no physical building obviously brings the costs down significantly.

For many other church planting models, money really does help. Typically, costs might include paying for staff, especially for a church leader, and their team as the church grows; for venue hire or upkeep; for equipment like sound systems, chairs, and musical instruments; and for other ministry costs like Bibles, children's materials, website, refreshments, signage, etc.

For a number of church planting models, the planter moves with his or her family and a team of four to six other people, and starts from scratch, finding local jobs to cover costs, then establishing and growing the church until the giving of the church is large enough to support staffing and other costs. One church planter tells the story of starting their church in a new city with some friends. They started four small groups which they all belonged to, to give each group a critical mass of its own, meeting Monday to Thursday. As people were invited and joined them, they started to focus on one group each. Then, when all four groups were big enough, they started to meet together to worship. It was only at that point that they needed money for venue hire. And once that started growing, they were able to pay for the leaders to go full time.

If you start with funding, then you face the question of what you fund first. The French language plant at St Barnabas Kensington uses existing facilities and funds its own French-speaking pastor. Mosaic Church in Harrow was run by a full-time GP and the costs were low to begin with. As the church grew, they began to raise funds to support a part-time leader to help with the growing organisational needs. At the other end of the scale, the HTB network uses a parish revitalisation model that has a small staff team from day one, often using and developing existing church buildings. This particular model is much more expensive, but they

5 https://www.facebook.com/forestchurchbournville/.

experience fast growth too as they reach de-churched and unchurched people in very effective ways.

The 'nuts and bolts'

In order to run smoothly, you need to create the financial systems and controls to enable the church plant to be efficient and effective at managing its money. This will help mitigate financial risks, comply with legal duties, corporate governance, and due diligence requirements, and meet your financial objectives. It is therefore extremely helpful to have a financially minded person on the team who can take care of this. They will need to develop a budget and manage it. They will need to work out how any money is going to be handled and recorded. The leader will usually need to take responsibility for raising the funds. And they will need to have an eye on how this is going to be sustained in the future – which means developing a culture of generosity and working out how to communicate about all aspects of the finances to the church. So let's run through these one by one.

Having a money person

Financial accountability is essential if you are handling money, and it is helpful to have a healthy separation between those who preach about the money and those who spend it. It is therefore helpful to have someone responsible, other than the lead planter, for the day-to-day finances. I find it helpful to think about two functions here – someone who oversees the money and someone or several people who handle it day to day. They could be the same in smaller plants, but as the church grows and the finances increase, the competence necessary might come in the form of a volunteer in the finance industry taking the role of treasurer and then a small team of people who count money, record it, and bank it.

I had the privilege of having Jacquie Driver as our treasurer in Shadwell. She was a qualified accountant and KPMG partner and did a brilliant job setting up systems and structures for our finances. She has since set up a charity that supports smaller churches with their finance systems to ease the burden of the increasing legal accountability that is now required with charities. We met regularly, usually fortnightly, to run through any financial decisions and for me to know where we stood with our bank balance. I remember Sandy Millar telling me in no uncertain terms, you need to know whether you are in the black or the red otherwise there will be trouble! Having this regular meeting meant that we always knew where we were financially, but also we could work out when we needed to be praying for more money and when we needed to ask the congregation to give more.

The treasurer should be responsible for all financial systems – setting them up and managing them on a regular basis.

Receiving and recording money

If you need financial independence from your sending church, you will need your own bank account. This might require having a holding account or a clear budget line in the sending church accounts, so that money can be allocated and spent as needed before the plant launches. As soon as the new bank account is set up, and this can take months, funds can then be transferred. If you want to receive tax back on any donations, you need to become a charity (more information later in this chapter) which will also take time.

It is vital to work out the financial systems before you plant, so have your finance person train everyone who needs to know the required procedures. Think through how money is received – through bank transfers, cash, etc – and what the processes are for banking it, always involving more than one person. All transactions need to be recorded in some way. If there are only a few transactions, then a simple spreadsheet is adequate, where entries can be matched with a bank statement. As the number and type of transactions grows more sophisticated, a more comprehensive system will be required. Getting this right will help give you a clear idea of your cash flow across the year; help you manage your financial resources and prioritise payments; ensure the church plant is organisationally efficient – rather than getting bogged down in financial chaos; and prevent fraud, whether from a staff member or volunteer, or from online theft.

IMPRINT Church, planted in Leicester and London, needed to agree spending limits and practices for each of their church ministry activities and their team leaders. This involved the leaders working out what would work in practice and then training everyone involved so they were all used to handling the money well. This was all coordinated by a treasurer who also had a small team supporting and helping him.

Budgeting and reporting

An essential skill for a church planter is understanding the plant's budget and how the accounts are reported – usually in an annual report, which covers the previous year, and management accounts, which are up-to-date monthly reports.

Before you create a budget, you need to work out what you want to do and how much it will cost. You should then prioritise these items into must-haves and nice-to-haves. Organise them into ministry areas and itemise them, line by line, in a spreadsheet. Then identify income streams – congregational giving, start-up grants, etc – and itemise them in the same spreadsheet. Do the maths to work out income vs expenditure. If it doesn't balance, remove the nice-to-haves. If it still doesn't balance, you need to find some more money or reduce your expenditure. You will need to take the time to make sure the budget is easy to read, understand, and easy to explain to others. This helps vision casting and fundraising as people can see what you are trying to do and how much you need.

Management accounts help you know where you stand financially at any particular point in the year. They usually include a profit and loss statement and a balance sheet. I quite like to see these using the same lines as the budget so it is clear what has been spent and what hasn't. This will have monthly expenditure, year-to-date total expenditure, and the budgeted expenditure.

These are then all assembled into year-end accounts that are presented in an Annual Report at an annual general meeting ('Annual Parochial Church Meeting' or 'APCM' in Anglican Churches). This follows standard practice for charities, which includes the annual Trustees Report, a narrative summarising key information about the church plant and its achievements; the annual financial accounts; and an Independent Examiner's Report (or auditor's report if applicable), offering an independent assessment of the financial reporting and situation of the church.

The reason I have spent so much time addressing finances is because many church planters are over-optimistic about giving in the short term and don't plan for financial sustainability in the medium to long term. This is alleviated by careful planning and being realistic about money, while remaining dependent on God. My encouragement to the church planter is to get some training in this area so you learn to appreciate how useful these tools can be and learn to steward the finances well.[6]

Fundraising

Fundraising is an essential quality for a church planter. In order to raise new funds, the planter needs to call the church to prayer and discern under God where best to source the funds. This might be by waiting, if that is what is discerned, or by asking for and seeking funds. I divide fundraising sources into four categories:

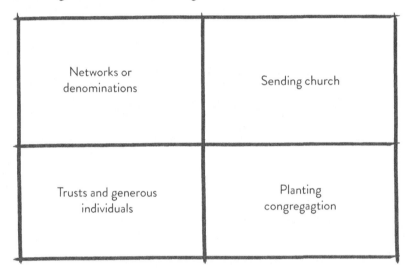

Figure 16: Sources of church planting funding

1. **Network or denominational sources** – If church planting is part of the wider vision and strategy then funding might be sourced from central denominational funds. Larger trusts and funders sometimes prefer to give to wider bodies like this to incentivise them to this kind of mission and to avoid having to decide on individual requests, leaving this to the central structures. Find out early what funds might be available, how to apply to them, and the likelihood of receiving the funding.

6 For more, see www.stewardship.org.uk.

2. **Sending church funding** – Churches that believe in church planting often have started to allocate and save money in their budgets for this. I actively encourage this as the first step in planting churches – it's putting your money where your mouth is! Have a conversation with the leader and treasurer of the sending church about how much can be expected and the requirements of receiving the grant. Sometimes churches have an offering on a final Sunday before the launch. This is a wonderful opportunity for one-off gifts and generosity from the sending church. Obviously, this is more difficult to predict and I would advise not including this in any budget.

3. **Planting congregation giving** – Part of the essential preparation for team members is to encourage them to give to the plant. The lead planter has to lead the way and set an example in this. Once they have given, it is easier for everyone to encourage new people to give because they have given themselves. This is part of cultivating generosity in the congregation – see below. Most of the finances in the future of the plant will come from this congregation as it grows.

4. **Other trusts and generous individuals** – There are a range of Christian charities that support church planting or aspects of church ministry that fit with a plant's remit. This might include having a youth worker or encouraging a particular historic link with evangelism or restoring a historic building. God may draw you to wealthy people who have a vision to support church planting. Be ready with your elevator pitch to describe the vision of what you are trying to do and what you need to proceed.

I have seen the way God provides in miraculous and generous ways, especially when we have prayed and brought our financial needs before him. We have received national funding for church planting in my home diocese of London on several occasions, trust funding for groups of church plants from a number of Christian trusts, and funds from wealthy Christians who have wanted to invest in the kingdom through church planting.

St Margaret's Portsmouth have a wonderful story of God's financial provision. When Fran Carabott was first asked to revitalise St Margaret's, the church had been shut and deemed unsafe. They began to meet in a community hall, and all the leaders of the church were volunteers. Their sending church gave them a budget of £6,000 to plant. God was so faithful that they never needed to use this money. People started to give towards their vision of building community with Jesus at the centre. The archdeacon visited, saw God's good work, and found funding for Fran to be paid to lead the church half-time. He then received a training grant from St Mellitus College, so that he could be trained for ministry. They soon outgrew the community hall and needed a larger space. God provided for that too. The church received funding from the Church of England to renovate the original St Margaret's Church building where they now meet. It is always encouraging, joyful, faith-building, and courage-building to see God pour out funds for church planting. Start praying, discerning, and seeking the funding God wants for you.

Encouraging a culture of generosity

Martin Luther once said, 'There are three conversions necessary: the conversion of the heart, the mind, and the purse.' Giving financially does not come naturally to us, perhaps because it can have such a hold on our hearts. St Paul described the love of money as 'a root of all kinds of evil.'[7] Giving is an essential part of discipleship and it can be cultivated as a spiritual discipline through encouragement, good teaching, and practical opportunities. How can we encourage giving within our church plants?

I think it is important to differentiate between the financial needs of a plant and the giving of a congregation. The latter will almost certainly be the major solution to the former. But sometimes God calls us to step out in faith beyond the giving of the existing congregation by providing through other means. That then means we depend on God to provide for us, through any means. And maturity comes when the congregation, through their one desire to give generously and take responsibility for the mission and ministry of the church, choose to pay all that is necessary. Sometimes this works the other way round too. There was one particular year in Shadwell when our treasurer Jacquie told us that 40 per cent of the church's income was being given to church planting. The church was desperate to give funds to enable other churches to be planted to reach new people with the gospel well beyond their own needs.

7 1 Timothy 6:10.

To enable this kind of culture of generosity, we need to teach into it. We see Paul in 2 Corinthians 8–9 stirring up the hearts of the early church to give financially to the poor in other churches. He reminded them of the sacrificial generosity of those in Macedonia who, despite persecution and poverty, had begged Paul for the chance to give. As we teach generosity, we must give people practical ways to start the journey of giving. In the Old Testament, there were various laws and practices for giving a proportion of income to temple worship and to the poor. In the New Testament, we are encouraged to give from our hearts, determining in advance what to give: 'Each of you should give what you have decided in your heart to give, not reluctantly or under compulsion, for God loves a cheerful giver.'[8]

I believe that we don't teach our congregations enough about money – earning it, giving it, saving it, spending it – and many have never been taught about any of these. No wonder many churches have such low incomes. Jesus recognised how important it was to teach about money. Sixteen of his 38 parables concern how to handle money and possessions. Ten per cent of verses in the Gospels deal directly with the subject of money. So we must teach in our preaching and also in our small groups what Jesus had to say about money. Explain why giving is so important, why it is beneficial to the giver, and how to give – both to church and for other kingdom purposes. Then have easy-to-use mechanisms for people to give to the church. Finally, you can then talk about the needs of the church – its upkeep, its staffing needs, and its mission opportunities.

I have heard some great ideas for encouraging people to give, like starting on a giving ladder – giving a percentage of your income to the church, starting with 1 per cent, then increasing it a percentage point per year. Others have clearly presented pie charts to explain where the money goes, so people know what they're giving to. I love how John Wesley, an Anglican priest and founder of the Methodist movement, never taught or practised tithing, that is giving away 10 per cent of one's income. Instead, after his own needs were met, he shared the rest, giving away 80 per cent of his income! I started giving at university and I can honestly say that it has been an extraordinary adventure in trusting God for ourselves and for the church.

Separately to this essential discipleship teaching on giving and money, schedule vision days – we have used two per year in September and

8 2 Corinthians 9:7.

February – at the beginning of the school year when new people often join churches and near the beginning of the calendar year – to recast the vision of the church, showing them how they can be involved in the vision, practically and financially. Then present the congregation with the opportunity to give to the vision, being clear about what the money is going to and how much is needed. Many of us have learned the principle that money follows vision and not the other way around. People get inspired to give when they understand the vision and their hearts are touched by it, they see the part they can play in the midst of it, and they feel they want to give financially to it as a way of being personally invested in it. So teach on giving regularly, tell stories of giving, and recommend books on giving. Cast the vision. Schedule opportunities to give to the vision. Then make it as easy as possible to give, thinking through and working through what is going to work best for your church community.

BECOMING A CHARITY

Many smaller church plants will not need to consider becoming a charity in their own right. They might be linked to a bigger church, coming under their charitable objects, or be part of a network that is held together by a charitable organisation. Some don't need to be a charity at all. So why mention it here? I think there are three main considerations: liability, credibility, and fundability.

If a church has an income of more than £100,000 it has to register as a charity by law. This threshold might well decrease in coming years. Most church plants will start under that. To be an independent entity, able to advertise themselves in the community and run public events, whether worship or otherwise, a church plant is treated as an unincorporated association with trustees. Liability for anything going wrong falls on the trustees individually, regardless of whether they are registered or not. By registering as a charity, specifically a charitable incorporated organisation (CIO), the plant is regarded as a separate legal entity, so contracts are with the church and not with individuals.

Becoming a CIO deals with questions about accountability, as regular reporting to the Charity Commission is required. In terms of credibility, church plants sometimes apply for grant funding, either from other charities or for community activities, and some funders only fund registered charities. Being registered as a charity is also helpful for getting a bank account because it gives confidence to banks that proper accountability structures are in place. Be aware that it can take several months to prepare your application to the Charity Commission, and longer for them to process, so this is worth getting on with at an early stage if you need to, and to approach potential trustees.

If you are revitalising a parish church, it is already a charity and should also have a bank account, but redesignating signatories can take time too. Make sure you have alternative financial cover while you are waiting for bank accounts and charitable status to clear. I have known some churches needing to wait six months and not being able to spend money already allocated to them because the waiting or the structures were not in place for easily accessing what was already theirs.

COACHING AND MENTORING

The practice of coaching has taken off in many sectors and the church has been slow to catch on, usually relegating it to 'people with problems who need that extra bit of help.' This is unfortunate because we are missing out on a hugely beneficial resource. A coach is able to ask objective questions about how you are preparing and developing the plant and its team. They do not need to be experts in planting, but having a core understanding of the process is helpful. I differentiate a coach from a mentor, who I would define as an expert who shares their knowledge, skills, and experience to help you develop and grow; someone who is able to guide you through the various questions and considerations of planting because they have done it themselves. On the other hand, coaches can be an unbiased guide, holding the planter to account for the goals they have already set for themselves and helping them reach their full potential.

We insist on plant leaders in our diocese having a coach and doing the training in order to give the maximum support that we can to each planter and their team. Of the more than 100 plants in our diocese, the ones that have engaged fully with this have led to stronger and more secure church plants and it is obvious the difference coaching has made.

COMMUNICATIONS

Having good communications systems and structures is vital to being organised and making sure the core messages of what you are trying to do reach the right people at the right time. We looked at how to best engage stakeholders in chapter 3. The planning tool there addressed who your stakeholders are and how you plan to communicate with them. This quickly becomes complex as the number of stakeholders increases and the messaging to each becomes more sophisticated. Managing these relationships, and keeping on top of communicating with them, needs a system. However basic this may sound, you need to work out who you want to communicate with, what you want to say to them, and how you are going to say it. This will involve a variety of face-to-face meetings, phone calls, individual and group emails, the church website, social media posts, noticeboards, and other written materials. It is also helpful to distinguish between internal and external communications at various levels: internal to members of the church, and external to those you are trying to reach or the community at large; but also private or perhaps confidential meetings with senior leaders and wider messages to local churches.

The important thing here is to keep track of these communications and appoint someone to look after this area. Increasingly, the first port of call for visitors to a church is its website. Make sure it says what you want it to say (your vision, values, policies including safeguarding, legal set-up, map, and events diary) and include the address of the church and easy ways to communicate with you. Although it may seem a little dated, for many churches the noticeboard is another critical tool. People walk past it every day, so make sure it is clear and well-maintained – if it isn't, that still communicates something about you! In other places, Instagram and dedicated WhatsApp groups might be the best way to communicate with a community.

Social media is a powerful tool. Resource church leader Hannah Patton uses it to engage with a great range of people at St John's Goole. She says:

> We've set up some local groups on Facebook like Goole Community Group and Goole Families and we post content on these, so we're getting a lot of fringe people engaging. Facebook is big here and everyone is 'friends' with each other, so the content gets shared a lot. We also made some clips about

mental health and parenting, which led to a number of people coming to 'Sunday Night at 8,' and some of them have gone on to do Alpha.[9]

Used well, social media can bring your message to a much broader audience.

Perhaps the most important communication tool is your members. Friends and family will respond to invitations because they trust them and see the difference that Jesus makes to their lives. Church members will be more confident to invite people if they themselves have a clear idea of the church's vision and structures and they believe in them. Identify the evangelists in the congregation and ensure they have everything they need to invite others. In practice, they will do most of the inviting, and as they do that, others will grow in confidence too.

I would really recommend looking back at your list of stakeholders and considering, how will you communicate with them, and how often? What is the basic information you need on a website? And, how might you use social media to spread news of the new plant?

IT SYSTEMS

Rather than spend too much time here outlining different IT solutions, which doubtless will be out of date in a few months, I encourage you to carefully consider how your IT systems will serve your vision. Consider questions such as:

- Do you have a system that will help you keep in touch with members of your church and hold their data securely? Have you built in capacity for growth?

- If you need a website, is it simple to update?

- Do you need an email system linked to your website that can handle multiple names with the same address?

- Do you need an internal communication system for your team?

- Do you need a separate finance accounting package which will integrate the finances/payroll and keep track of expenditure?

9 St John's Goole now has different worshipping patterns, but the principle of good communications still applies.

Your sending church almost certainly has IT systems that are set up to manage these activities, but they may or may not be helpful for your plant which is probably going to be much smaller and require less expertise to run. The important thing here is to be clear about what you need. You can do this very cheaply or it can be extremely expensive, depending on your needs and church size. And there are some products that offer everything in one place which is obviously pretty helpful too. Shop around and get advice before you take the plunge!

TRACKING AND MEASUREMENT

When you planned your strategy using the Leader's Map in chapter 3, you might have set some goals. Tracking and measurement is simply a discipline to help you know how far you have got to achieving those goals. You can measure how many people are attending your meetings – that's an output measure resulting from the work you have done. You can also measure how many people you have invited to church – that's an input measure which results in people coming. Spending time developing input and output measurements will help you work out whether you are on track and whether you need to adapt your approach. You might not be a measurement type, but there might well be someone in the plant who is, or find a friend who might help. Wherever it comes from, investing in this area is extremely helpful and revealing for what works or not, and also for what can be celebrated as you reach milestones you have been aiming for. You might be surprised by some of the results.

A few years into our plant in Shadwell, another planter in our network, Jon March, developed a questionnaire that his congregation started to use for tracking – both understanding who was in the congregation at that point but also how it was changing year-on-year. We took his template and adjusted it to suit our own needs. We found it so helpful to work out more detail about who was actually in our congregation, and to get feedback from them too. We used the questionnaire over several years and did infographics for the congregation to see the results too. We asked what they appreciated about church, what needed to be better, and what subjects they wanted input on. We were also able to discover varying levels of spiritual maturity by asking when they had come to faith, whether they were in small groups, if they gave financially and how, and if they had invited anyone to the Alpha course or to church. There was so much we were able to discover that helped us better pitch our evangelism, discipleship, teaching, and training.

RESOURCES TOOLBOX

It is vital to identify a lead person who can take responsibility for each of these areas of ministry. They are so important that you need someone to coordinate them to ensure that they get done, and done well. All of these are possible with good volunteers, but as the plant grows some of this will require more financial resources, when you will need to balance having a staff member oversee some or all of these or outsource some of this work to a third party. Get these right though and you'll have a finely honed organisation that will save a lot of problems down the line.

CALL TO ACTION: RESOURCES

- What safeguarding policies and practices do you need in your church plant?
- Who is your safeguarding officer?
- How will the leaders enable your plant to be safe?
- Who will be your treasurer?
- What is your budget?
- What is your funding strategy?
- What is your governance structure?
- Who is coaching you?
- What are the key messages you are seeking to communicate? To whom?
- What will your rhythm be for different staff meetings (e.g. Sunday planning, yearly reviews/devotionals/highs and lows, etc)?
- What are you measuring to reach your goals?

9
IMPLEMENTATION

HOW TO LAUNCH, GROW, AND MULTIPLY YOUR PLANT

Athletes train for the beginning and early steps of races by visualising the perfect start. In addition to all their strength, fitness, and stamina training, they prepare for the start of the race. Lack of preparation can hold you back from giving your best. Good preparation builds confidence for the start and first stages of the race. It's the same with preparing the first stages of church planting in practice. How will you launch your plant? How will you grow it? How will you review progress? How might you multiply the plant to become many plants in the future?

LAUNCH

There is always a start date. When is your D-Day? When do you start in earnest? When do you start measuring things? Fixing a launch date focuses the mind and your preparations and helps everyone else know that it is actually going to happen. There are many ways to launch church plants, but they essentially fall into two categories – going large or starting slow.

Going large, or having a 'big bang' launch, is about letting everyone know, inviting as many as possible, and creating a critical mass of people present such that visitors have a chance to experience what coming back is going to feel like. Typically, larger plants take this approach, including church revitalisations where an intentional message to get out is, 'Come and check out the new thing that's happening.' This will probably be marked by a church service with worship, a talk, some kind of response, along with some social time to get to know one another. This takes a lot of energy and effort – a bit like a rocket launch – and leaves people in no doubt that it is a new thing that is going on. Church revitalisations in the Church of England have public services to which local dignitaries and community stakeholders are invited to witness the new incumbent being sworn in and being prayed for. This is a great opportunity to make a splash and invite people to the first Sunday services. This can be enhanced by leafleting the local area, putting up banners and notices, and knocking on people's doors. It's good news and people need to know!

When St Paul's, Harringay launched a new service as part of the graft from Christ Church Mayfair, they 'went large' with a big party. Nearly 70 adults attended the launch, which included children's activities, a service of blessing, and prayers jointly led by a new member of the church grafting team along with a longstanding member of the original St Paul's congregation. The launch marked a new beginning, a fresh start, a sign to the community around it that something new was happening and it was worth checking out!

Going slow is the opposite, taking time to immerse oneself into the local context – and is typical of how the Fresh Expressions movement has approached their planting. They begin by being present, intentionally listening to local people, finding ways to love them and serve them. As relationships develop, the planters build community, working out what best fits their needs and starting to be intentional about discipleship and sharing faith. When it is the right time, the church begins to take shape, slowly but surely, and taking into account the local context that might look very different to how a bigger church might have formed. The whole process is immersed and underpinned in prayer and connected to the wider church in the local area (see chapter 3 for more on this).

There are many ways in between these two approaches to consider. Some church plants have started with summer events, making connections with the local community, before launching gathered worship services. Others started with an evangelistic course, like the Alpha course, developed small groups off the back of the course and then, once there were enough groups to have a critical mass, brought them together to worship as a bigger gathering. Some churches have simply emerged unexpectedly – a church in Harrow had a thrift shop at one end of the parish. They offered coffee and prayer for customers and found they had regulars coming who wanted more. They hosted a carol service and found that there was demand for an Alpha course and the potential of a church emerged, reaching completely different people to those coming to the main parish building.

The Engine Room, Tottenham Hale, was planted into a purpose-built space at the bottom of a block of flats in a new housing development.

London City Missioners, Andrew and Martina, who were based there, hosted clubs and events that the community wanted and appreciated. After a year, a woman who came to one of their activities, said, 'I love this church.' They said, 'What do you mean? We don't have any services!' The woman said, 'You're Christians and when I come here I feel closer to God. So this is a church, right?' That was the sign to Andrew and Martina that they were ready to form a church, and public worship soon followed. Going slow was just the right pace for them.

There is no right way. Each approach depends on the local context and what is discerned as the best way. Keep asking questions about the context and how best to reach the people within it, then work out the kind of launch that is best. However you tailor your approach, make sure the whole team are on the same page and have the same expectations.

PUBLICITY

Publicising the church plant should be carefully considered. Who are you trying to target and how will you reach them? This will range from signage pointing towards the church site, through to online messaging. One church in Hampton Wick used Facebook advertising to reach particular groups in the community. For just a few pounds they advertised their family life courses and their Alpha course. I made a habit of asking every newcomer how they came to hear about the church and how they had come to be there. Some were walk-ins, some searched online for an Alpha course, or marriage and parenting courses, or simply for a local church, and some were invited by members. Knowing this can help you plan how to reach new people in a targeted and effective way. There are plenty of experts to ask for help in this area.

AS YOU GROW

If Day One of a church plant is the launch, Day Two is about encouraging the church to grow. Jesus talked about growth in many of his parables: like a mustard seed, a tiny seed of faith grows into a huge tree; he spoke of the importance of soil in which crops grow to 30, 60, 100 times what was sown; even a small amount of yeast influencing a huge batch of dough. God makes things grow but he calls us to work with him to achieve it. So what should we do to help our plant grow?

The Church Commissioners conducted some church growth research in 2013 and they found that certain churches and cathedrals stood out as having experienced significant growth. They concluded that, while there is no single recipe, there are common ingredients strongly associated with growth in churches of any size, place, or context. Here are the eight factors that stood out:

1. **Having a clear mission and purpose** – Growing churches are marked by having a clear vision for mission and growth. These churches align themselves and their activities with their vision, which is regularly communicated to their members so they are on mission together.

2. **Being intentional in prioritising growth** – It might be obvious, but if you say you want to grow, you are more likely to grow! Growing churches offer evangelistic courses and newcomers' meetings because they expect to grow and therefore prioritise it. They actively engage with those who don't go to church in as many ways as they can.

3. **Willingness to self-reflect, to change and adapt according to context** – Churches concerned with attracting new members are prepared to make changes to reach them without losing their purpose. They regularly assess what is working well or not and adjust accordingly.

4. **Involvement of lay members in leadership roles** – Growing churches are marked by significant training, development, and releasing of lay people, recognising that clergy have limited capacity.

5. **Actively engaging children and teenagers** – Most people come to faith as children, and stay in the faith if they are nurtured and supported as they grow up. Growing churches invest in children and youth work and attract their parents too.

6. **Cultivate a welcoming culture** – Treating visitors as potential members means these churches look to build ongoing relationships with people and follow up with all visitors to draw them into the life of the church.

7. **Being intentional in nurturing disciples** – Growing churches are interested in how individual disciples can grow, through small groups, courses, and time spent nurturing new and existing Christians.

8. **Good leadership** – Being intentional about developing high quality leadership strongly correlates with growing churches. Their leaders are marked by abilities to motivate, envision, and innovate in their contexts.

The findings are recorded in their report, *Anecdote to Evidence*, and this is an excellent resource to reflect on and apply to your own context.

The Gregory Centre has spent several years working with a range of sizes of church and different church traditions who want to grow but feel they need help doing so. Working with a learning community format, with six to 10 churches journeying together, the Grow Course[1] looks at how to grow deeper in their relationship with God, increase their impact on the local community, and grow numerically. They spend time looking at the church's role in:

- **Vocation** – What is the unique calling of your local church in its context and the calling of its leadership to serve that church in particular?

- **Formation** – How can disciples be best formed in that context so they can be effective witnesses to Jesus Christ in the world around them?

- **Mission** – What are the opportunities for evangelism and witness in the neighbourhood and with relationships, and how can they be enhanced and developed?

- **Multiplication** – How can disciples, groups, and congregations be multiplied to see the church grow? This includes planting new congregations and churches.

There are a number of other practical approaches that churches are finding useful, like Partnership for Missional Church,[2] developed and run by

1 https://ccx.org.uk/grow-course/.
2 https://churchmissionsociety.org/partnership-for-missional-church/.

the Church Mission Society, and Leading your Church into Growth,[3] developed by Robin Gamble with a diverse delivery team from a range of churches and traditions. No matter which approach you take, the most important starting point is to want to grow and to invest time and energy into praying and actively seeking it. Day Two is growing the church plant!

REVIEW YOUR PROGRESS

Once you have launched your plant, and it is beginning to grow, how will you know what is really going on? You need to create some kind of system that will help you to review how the plant is progressing. The simplest way to do this is to use an existing system and adapt it to your own needs.

So what might this look like? Effective organisations have used action learning processes to be intentional at being as effective as possible in what they are called to do. We used a form of this in our services and strategy meetings. The structure is simple – looking back, what worked well, what didn't, why was this, what are we going to do about it, and then making it happen. This follows the action learning cycle:

1. **Plan** – Make a plan, whether it's a Sunday service, or an Alpha course, or a prayer meeting, or a community gathering. Include a follow-up meeting to review it.

2. **Act** – Make it happen, doing what you'd planned to do.

3. **Reflect** – When you review what you have done, ask what worked and what didn't, and how it went according to plan.

4. **Learn** – Ask why it worked or didn't and work through how it could be improved for next time. You might choose to stop it as a result.

5. **Plan again** – Build the reflections and learning into the next plan and continue in the cycle.

3 https://www.leadingyourchurchintogrowth.org.uk/.

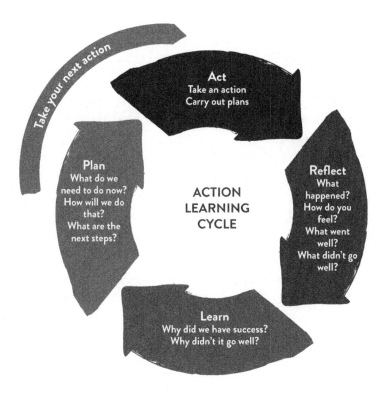

Figure 17: The action learning cycle

Sometimes it's good to capture the reflections immediately after the event from everyone involved which gives a slightly different and more immediate perspective, but this should not replace a more measured reflection and learning moment a day or so later.

Action learning is good to cultivate as a discipline for regular and semi-regular events and practices. It helps you focus on continual improvement and keeps you humble as you keep learning from your mistakes! Sometimes we need to be honest with ourselves and others and even accept that the vision for a plant, while we still believe it is from God, may not be for this time or this place, and we need to lay it down, or pass it on to others to take it to the next stage.

MULTIPLICATION

The principle of multiplication runs through church planting. What if we didn't just plant a church, but planted a church that plants churches that plants churches? What if we don't just encourage discipleship, but make disciples who make disciples who make disciples? What if we don't just develop leaders, but develop a whole pipeline of leaders? There is a simple decision to move from an 'addition' mindset to a 'multiplication' one, and that decision transforms our aspirations and our outcomes.

We see this principle operating throughout Scripture. In Genesis chapter one, God made a fruitful world that is designed to grow and reproduce. His first words to human beings are 'Be fruitful and increase in number.'[4] Jesus didn't just teach parables about growth in the kingdom, he also taught the principle of multiplication. He talked about sowing seeds that produced a crop up to 100 times what was sown.[5] His command to make disciples of all nations has involved a multiplication from the 12 apostles to hundreds of millions of followers. The church in Antioch effectively planted churches all over Europe through multiple phases of the apostle Paul's planting, as well as other planting by other apostolic leaders like Barnabas and Silas. And we have seen, in chapter 7, how the church in Ephesus was responsible for churches being planted all over the province of Asia over a short period of time.

If you make one disciple each year for 10 years, you get 10 new disciples. If you make a disciple and train them to make disciples each year, you get 512 new disciples after 10 years (see the table on the next page)! Now, I know it doesn't always work that way: there are fruitful and less fruitful seasons; fellow Christians struggle and sometimes lapse. But making disciple-makers multiplies your discipleship efforts in a completely different way to discipling others, as good as that is.

4 Genesis 1:28.
5 Matthew 13:8; Mark 4:20; Luke 8:8.

Year	Y1	Y2	Y3	Y4	Y5	Y6	Y7	Y8	Y9	Y10
Make a disciple each year:	1	2	3	4	5	6	7	8	9	10
Make a disciple each year who makes disciples:	1	2	4	8	16	32	64	128	256	512

In the same way, if you plant a church every three years for 12 years, you get four plants. If you plant a church-planting church every three years, you get eight plants. Do it over 24 years and you get 128 churches! The difference is simply training the church planter to identify and train someone else and ask that church planter to do the same.

Year	Y3	Y6	Y9	Y12	Y15	Y18	Y21	Y24
Plant a church every three years:	1	2	3	4	5	6	7	8
Plant a church-planting church every three years:	1	2	4	8	16	32	64	128

I would love to see these principles applied across the Church. Imagine what might follow!

Studies show that church plants gain around a quarter to two-thirds of their new members from the ranks of people who are not attending any worshipping body, and are more effective at reaching beyond the existing boundaries of the church than more established churches.[6] And churches can continue to be planted in different ways to reach different people in different places. A parish church doesn't just need to have one congregation or one place of worship. It could have multiple congregations in multiple places to reach the multiple groups of people within that single area. What we actually need is fewer declining churches, and many more growing ones!

As soon as you start applying this multiplication principle to church planting, you also start to benefit from economies of scale and lightness of touch to see churches planted in multiples rather than just in ones or twos. In Shadwell, having planted in 2005, and gone on to revitalise four other churches with planting teams, we began to start thinking about how we could plant more churches, raise up more planting leaders and teams, and develop practices that made it easier to plant. Holy Trinity Brompton, at the heart of the HTB network, has developed 'Accelerator' training for many church planters at once, and not just from their own church, and this has seen a significant increase in the number of plants it sends each year, while also encouraging their own plants to plant again.

Churches and networks that begin to start thinking like this and making it happen in practice are beginning to create a 'church planting movement', when the vision of churches planting churches spreads from the original planter into the churches themselves, so that in their very nature they are planting churches and reproducing themselves.[7]

---

6 Recent studies show church planting is most effective at reaching unchurched and de-churched people. For example, The Church Army's Research Unit found that 60 per cent of attendees of Messy Church are unchurched and de-churched, see *Playfully Serious: How Messy Churches Create New Space for Faith* (2019). One study shows that 60 per cent of attendees of Fresh Expressions are de-churched and unchurched: https://churcharmy.org/wp-content/uploads/2021/04/the-day-of-small-things.pdf. Another study reports that this number is 29 per cent: https://www.churchofengland.org/sites/default/files/2022-03/fresh-expressions-of-church-fruitfulness-framework-report-eido-research-1.pdf. In one study, newly planted Resource churches had an average attendance of over 400, with 23 per cent unchurched and de-churched people in their congregations: www.churchofengland.org/sites/default/files/2021-05/topic-summary-new-resource-churches.pdf. Also see, Tim Keller, 'Church Planting', delivered at the London Church Planting Consultation, September 2008, 5.

7 Church Planting Movements (CPM) are usually defined as rapid, exponential, and indigenous. I have broadened that definition here. See for example, www.missionfrontiers.org.

So as you plan your launch and create the structures for action learning, start to pray for multiplication by planning for the next plant. And the one after that. And the one after that!

Training church planters

I have enjoyed studying the apostle Paul's developing practices in Acts, across each of the journeys, and in particular the third journey and his leadership in Ephesus. Luke writes, 'Paul . . . took the disciples with him and had discussions daily in the lecture hall of Tyrannus. This went on for two years, so that all the Jews and Greeks who lived in the province of Asia heard the word of the Lord.'[8] I often ask myself how did everyone in Asia, that is the western third of modern-day Turkey, hear the word of the Lord? It must have been through church planting throughout the region. How do I surmise that? The letters to each of the churches in Revelation 2–3 were all planted during this season, that is Ephesus, Smyrna, Pergamum, Thyatira, Sardis, Philadelphia, and Laodicea, along with churches in Colossae and Hierapolis, that were planted by Epaphras.[9] Paul must have been training disciples as church planters in the hall of Tyrannus in Ephesus and then sent them out to plant churches all over the region in just a two to three year period. This is highly intentional and clearly very productive.

We don't know what the curriculum in the hall of Tyrannus was, but it led to a multiplying, Christ-centric, church planting movement that transformed a whole region with the gospel. To train church planters today, I wonder if it is less about what is specifically on the curriculum – because there are some excellent colleges and Bible schools – and more about the expectations of making disciples, apprenticing church planters, launching new churches, and praying for a whole region to be transformed.

The simplest way to plant a church-planting church is by adding an apprentice church planter to the planting team. The apprentice is being trained by the church planter, learning on the job, and reflecting on the experience.[10] The apprentice would begin to start planning their own

8 Acts 19:9–10.
9 Colossians 1:7; 4:12–13.
10 See Christian Selvaratnam, *The Craft of Church Planting: Exploring the Lost Wisdom of Apprenticeship* (London: SCM, 2022).

church plant, gathering a new team, and planning to plant themselves. When they are ready, they plant out from the first plant. At that point, the new church planter would take on their own new apprentice, and the first church planter would take on a new apprentice planter too. We have come to call this 'planting pregnant,' because when you plant you have the 'embryo' of the next plant already in the team in the person of the apprentice planter!

In the same way, I want to encourage you not just to plant a church but to plant a church-planting church. Plant with a view that you will go on to plant other churches that will plant other churches and so on. This leads to a completely different approach and hugely different potential impact. The way you can do this is by identifying an apprentice who you can train on the job until they are ready to go themselves.

Creating a culture of multiplication

As you begin to think through the theology of multiplication in your own context, there are many applications that you can use to increase the impact you can make. The more widely you apply it, the more it begins to change the culture and DNA of what you are doing. Consider using some of the following:

- Preach about church members going on a church planting team, giving away your best, getting ready to step up after a plant.

- Develop an intern scheme to create a future pipeline of leaders.

- Help ordinands to grow in disciple-making and leadership development.

- Use curates to plant a new worshipping community and train leaders to take it on once they move on themselves.

- Recruit apprentice planters for planting or getting ready for a future plant.

- Model co-leadership in every aspect of church life – welcoming, serving, using the PA, co-leading services.

- Take an apprentice leader with you when you travel.

DEVELOPING A LONG TERM APPROACH

The early months and years of planting a new worshipping community are so exciting, challenging, and rewarding. To see people coming to faith in Jesus and growing as disciples is one of the greatest privileges I have ever experienced. Week by week, faithful ministry bears fruit over time. Year on year, you will see God doing extraordinary things in your church and through your church. What might happen over a generation if the plant keeps growing in maturity and impact? Pray, not just for this week, but also for the long term impact. Don't just work out a five-year strategy, develop a 25-year strategy. It might outlast you, but that kind of vision and strategy will go further than your wildest dreams!

CALL TO ACTION: IMPLEMENTATION

- When is the launch date?
- What is the appropriate launch strategy? Going big or going slow?
- Do you have a clear mission and purpose? What are they?
- How are you being intentional in prioritising growth?
- How will you nurture a disciple-making culture?
- Who is your apprentice?
- Who is your next church planter?
- Set dates in the diary to review how things are going.

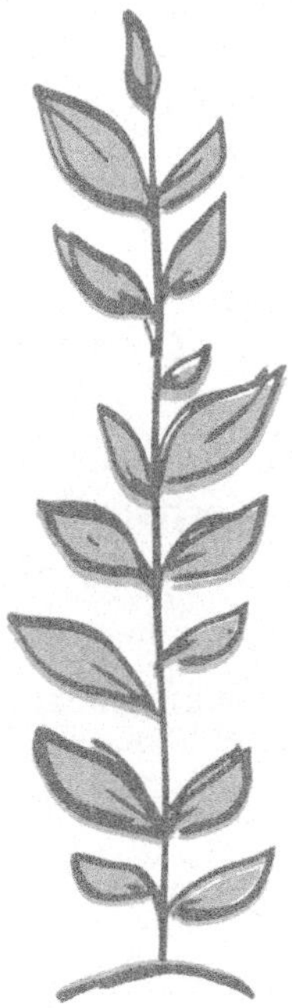

CONCLUSION

My office sits in the shadow of St Paul's Cathedral. This magnificent building has sat proudly as a Christian witness in the heart of the City of London for hundreds of years. It is dear to my heart, not least because I am fortunate enough to be a prebendary and have a bishop's stall in it. As an engineer by training, I also treasure it for the fascinating story of its construction. In particular, we can learn some crucial lessons about church planting from its architect, Sir Christopher Wren.

As you may know, St Paul's emerged from a catastrophe. In 1666, the Great Fire of London destroyed the old cathedral along with 13,000 houses, important civic buildings, and 87 churches in the City. Wren stepped forward and effectively said, 'I've got a vision for something which is going to be greater than what was there before. Let's rebuild St Paul's Cathedral, and let's also rebuild all the lost churches and the beating heart of this city.' It was a massive vision, for something bigger and better than what went before.

Wren needed to develop ways of communicating this vision so that people would buy into it. Crucially, he needed to bring King Charles II on board; he would be a key donor and would influence other benefactors. Wren knew he needed to catch people's attention, and ignite their imagination. So instead of simply drawing sketches of his vision, he hired specialist model builders and spent a year constructing a model which in his day cost the equivalent of a London townhouse. The result was a spectacular vision of a building that must have looked like a futuristic dream.

However, Wren designed a dome in the model which was thought to be impossible to replicate on the actual building. The understanding of physics and architecture required to build the cathedral's dome simply did not exist at the time. There was no known way in which the dome would support the weight of the roof. But Wren said, 'Let's just start in faith and we'll work it out as we go along.' He and his team started the project, knowing that they had to solve the problem as they went along.

Here's where Robert Hooke, physicist and friend of Wren, steps in. Hooke had discovered that significant weight could be hung on a chain, made stronger by the tension of the parabolic (pointy) arc. Together, they realised that the parabolic arc could be flipped over to point upwards, and made it from stone. This innovation bred new innovation. They decided to have three domes. There would still be the outer, shielding the cathedral from the elements, and the inside dome, for interior decoration. However, they would also build a hidden inner dome between the two, which was strong enough to hold the weight of the lantern. Wren could keep the beautiful design on the inside and outside, and also support the vast weight of the lantern. Together, they had solved the problem.

This story inspires and encourages us as we prepare to plant churches. Wren had a vision. He kept it in mind at all times, and clearly communicated it to others, through investing time and money in his model. Spend time discerning and articulating your vision. Find ways to communicate it to others in creative ways. Keep coming back to this vision each and every day, so that when you're concentrating on the day-to-day work before you, you can keep your eyes fixed on the big picture. Let this story of vision, innovation, and teamwork shape and inspire your work each day.

If you feel that God is calling you to start a church, trust his call and know you'll find the answers on the way. Wren knew he had to begin building St Paul's, even though the design was thought to be impossible. He trusted God and started laying stone. We may have a vision for a church plant which seems impossible. People may be telling you that it can't be done. If God has given you a vision, trust that you will find the answers, and discover new ways to make the impossible possible.

Finally, you need partners to make it possible. In the story of St Paul's, innovation was borne out of friendship. If Wren and Hooke were not companions on this journey, they would have never discovered how to build the dome. Surround yourself with partners in the gospel, friends, family, and colleagues who share your vision. Encourage them and be encouraged by them. Let your planting ministry emerge from your companionship.

Now is the time to plant! Missionary frontiers today are here in the UK, on our own doorsteps. I pray you will use this book as a practical guide to help you move from vision to reality. Most importantly, pray earnestly for the gift of the Holy Spirit, to strengthen and guide you as you follow his call in the world.

APPENDIX: WHO PLANTS CHURCHES?

Below are some of the attributes or qualities that are often recognised in church planters and pioneers. It is not a profile as such, or an exhaustive list, but rather an indicator of the type of person that would thrive in a church planting/pioneering environment.

Which of these qualities do you see in yourself or in others known to you?

A NATURAL STARTER

- A track record of starting new things; has established a pattern of innovation or 'firsts' in life and/or ministry.

- A sense of call to starting a new church or worshipping community.

- A sense of 'holy dissatisfaction' with the current and the need for something new to accomplish God's mission.

- A sense of call to a particular community, culture, or people group.

- A willingness, boldness, and faith to do something untried; ability to visualise a new church or worshipping community, that does not yet exist, through faith.

- An entrepreneurial spirit – resilient in the face of failure, curious to explore alternatives. Sees failure as a learning opportunity and step up to the next thing.

- Can courageously take the next step, without the full revelation of the way ahead.

A LEADER

- Casts a bold vision; leads and influences others into this reality.

- Takes others on a journey towards a common purpose.

- Demonstrates a flair for engaging, enabling, and mobilising others – makes things happen and drives momentum.

- Generates other leaders; trains and equips others to lead in order to multiply ministry.

- Enables others to discover their own call and to operate out of their spiritual gifts and abilities.

- Leads self; maintains own emotional and physical well-being through challenging situations.

- Establishes credibility and has the confidence and conviction to make others want to follow.

A GATHERER

- Gathers people and builds a team readily (volunteers and staff).

- Comes up with ideas that others are keen to adopt and implement.

- Resourceful and makes creative use of the resources available.

- Makes the ask and raises funds to support initiatives and ministry.

A FAITH SHARER

- Easily builds rapport with people outside the church or on the fringes.

- Communicates the Christian faith naturally to those outside the Church.

- Helps people come to faith and grow in faith.

- Effectively builds relationships. Initiates meeting people and deepening relationships as a basis for effective ministry.

A HEART FOR MISSION

- Identifies and readily responds to missional opportunities.

- Passionate about the extension and growth of God's kingdom; 'Missio Dei.'

- Recognises that fruitful mission is directly linked to spiritual practices (prayer, rest, solitude, sabbath, etc).

- Demonstrates rhythms of outreach and withdrawal; advance and retreat (ebb and flow).

- Has the capacity to sustain their own personal and spiritual life, through a relationship with God, and fund missionary energy and leadership.

- Has a spirituality that recognises the reality of struggle and opposition, and can draw on God's love and strength to overcome obstacles. Resilient in the face of adversity.

ABOUT THE AUTHOR

Ric Thorpe was appointed as Bishop of Islington in 2015 to oversee the Diocese of London's church planting and church growth work. He also serves the Church of England nationally, supporting bishops, dioceses, church planters, and pioneers, to develop church planting strategies and to plant new worshipping communities to reach new people in new places in new ways. He is the director of the Gregory Centre for Church Multiplication which offers church growth and church planting training and support for the full breadth of the Church. Ric served as Chair of the Fresh Expressions charity for five years, is Chair of the Gratitude Initiative, and is an assistant bishop in Southwark Diocese. He has a doctorate in church planting from Asbury Theological Seminary and is a tutor in church planting at St Mellitus College, London.

Before his current role, Ric and his wife Louie led a team from Holy Trinity Brompton to plant into St Paul's Shadwell in London's East End where they served for just over a decade. Over this time, the church went on to send four other planting and revitalisation teams to churches in the local area. Ric trained as a chemical engineer and worked in marketing with Unilever before joining the staff of Holy Trinity Brompton. Ric and Louie have three children and live in London. He loves deeply breathing sea air and taking in a long horizon, and better still, being out on the water in a sailing boat.

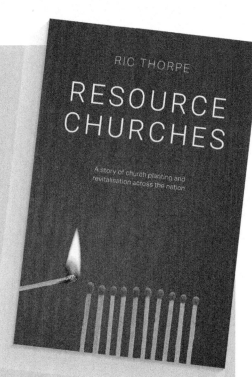

Written by Ric Thorpe, the Church of England's bishop for church planting, this book looks at the biblical, theological and historical roots of resource churches.

It covers all the practicalities of how to launch and grow an effective resource church, and draws on Ric's extensive experience, practical wisdom and advice for church teams and diocesan leaders.

It is full of stories from those who have planted and lead resource churches, together with reflections from each of their bishops. Although the book is written from an Anglican perspective, its principles may be applied to similar churches in other denominations and sections of the church.

For more information, scan the QR code or visit www.ccx.org.uk

The Gregory
Centre **for Church**
Multiplication